A SPIRITUAL ROADMAP

A SPIRITUAL ROADMAP

Walking the Path
in the Twenty-first Century

MICHAEL HEDLEY BURTON

STEINERBOOKS | 2016

STEINERBOOKS
An imprint of Anthroposophic Press, Inc.
610 Main St., Great Barrington, MA 01230
www.steinerbooks.org

Cover image: detail from the "red west window" by Rudolf Steiner in the Goetheanum, Dornach, Switzerland. Author photograph © by Katherine Burton. Book and cover design by Jens Jensen

Michael Burton can be contacted at
michaelburton@clear.net.nz

LIBRARY OF CONGRESS CONTROL NUMBER: 2016930295

ISBN: 978-1-62148-160-7 (paperback)
ISBN: 978-1-62148-161-4 (eBook)

Contents

Introduction: What Is the Path?

"I am being driven forward
into an unknown land.
The pass grows steeper,
the air colder and sharper.
A wind from my unknown goal
stirs the strings
of expectation.

Still the question:
will I ever get there?
There where life resounds,
a clear, pure note
in the silence."

—DAG HAMMARSKJÖLD, *Markings*[1]

The first dictionary I look at defines the word *path* as "a footway, track, or line along which a person or thing moves." A path as "something along which a person moves" is a convenient meaning from which to start. We all have our personal image of a path. For some it is made of cement and progresses in a disciplined straight line beside a busy highway; for others it is formed out of nothing more than the imprint of the feet of those who have walked on it and meanders along through wood or forest or field of ripening corn. There are many kinds of paths along which human beings may move.

But the path of the outer world is not the only kind of path. There is also an inner path—one along which one moves not in the world of the senses but among the goals and aspirations by which we set our course. It may be straight or crooked; similar to many other paths or unique; frequented by many or the place of a solitary wanderer. And it may change—it may go for a time through a densely populated city, then beside a river, then across a desert, then through a dangerous swamp, then in darkness with a steep drop on either side and then, like the path Dag Hammarskjöld describes above, it may become a steep, rocky pass among the mountain peaks. Some of those who walk it may give up, fall to their deaths or die of exhaustion; others make it to their destination, perhaps because they feel a "wind from [their] unknown goal" that "stirs the strings of expectation."

The phrase *walk the path* is a metaphor for the life journey lived by spiritual seekers and their steps taken toward illumination. Seekers who have resolved to become seers move progressively toward a goal, one that invariably recedes but nevertheless draws the seeker toward it. Today there are people all over the world—Christians, Buddhists, Muslims, as well as those who claim no allegiance to any of the world's religions—who would say they are on some kind of spiritual journey. Many examples could be given; the style of wandering of which I am personally most fond is that of the fifteenth-century initiate Christian Rosenkreutz. People who seek spiritual insight today read *The Chymical Wedding*[2]—his account of the seven days and nights that constituted his journey—not only for the very great wisdom and knowledge of spiritual processes contained in it, but also to encounter this most remarkable personality. We meet a man who has the qualities that enable him to withstand the many dangers and temptations that assail the spiritual seeker on his quest, so that he is able to attain his destination. The humanity and *goodness* of Christian Rosenkreutz stream out from the pages of the text in such a way that they can have a deep effect on those who read it.

This book is written for people who know (or at least have an inkling of this in their heart) that they are treading their individual path of life. These people are those who realize that they can never go the way of the herd—that pseudo-path, corrupted by another's will, which dictators and advertising executives do their best to induce everyone to travel. Instead of this, the people who I hope will work with this book are seeking to find the path that is most true to their particular emerging individuality. There is a road before them and they hope they are in possession of the strength and discrimination to move progressively along it. Some time ago, it happened; something set their steps moving in this particular direction, and they began to walk their path. It has become their life's journey.

If this is you, then you will also know how the real guidance is within. Your own road cannot be bypassed by substituting any other person's experience. Yet every person whom a traveler encounters can become a guide for a time if the traveler is able to accept messages from that person that are helpful and that resonate from the encounter.

There never has been an age quite like ours. The swirling confusion of our time demands that a few lights be shone onto it, and this book is a roadmap that does not spell out one single way but gives guidance concerning the terrain ahead in which the traveler will be journeying. People who are looking for marching orders that will guide them toward a fixed route are searching in vain. All wanderers must find their own way forward, but I hope that you (who have chosen to spend a little time with the author of the *Roadmap*) will conclude that you know the terrain ahead a little better than you would if you had not studied this book.

You can look on this book as you would a person whom you have met upon the road and with whom you choose to walk for a time. I am a traveler like you and these words are a rough guide, no more. They attempt to shine some light onto the spiritual conditions of the present age in the hope that this may help you on your life's journey. What is in this book is meant to be a stimulus to help you find your own voice and address your own questions. No one can solve these questions but you. Your path is unique, but as you walk it you need not always feel alone. There is no security on this path, no certainty about anything but the compass in your own heart.

May this little book be of some assistance to all who seek to find their path. I walk my path, just as you are walking yours—the path unique to those who strive to develop their truest individuality.

Summary of Introduction: What is the path?

The definition of the word *path* in the inner and outer worlds. Christian Rosenkreutz as the archetypal traveler on the path. How this book is written as a guide and stimulus for those who are walking their own individual life paths and to help readers find their own voice and address their most important questions and how only we as individuals can solve these questions.

The Starting Point

"The human being is not by any means of fixed and enduring form. He is much more an experiment and a transition...not yet a finished creation but rather a challenge of the spirit—a distant possibility, dreaded as much as it is desired."
—HERMANN HESSE, *Steppenwolf*[1]

M ost people alive in our time seem to understand that truth is not something that can be passed on ready-made from one person to another. A very wise person may teach you and might be able to give you facts and insights that greatly influence your life, but you must make truth your own. There is something within you that determines whether you are able to assimilate what you have been given and place it into a realistic relationship to the rest of your life.

The present age is a time of turmoil—an age between ages— a real turning of the tides. Signs of crisis are everywhere: world financial crisis, environmental destruction, vast numbers of refugees uprooted from their homelands, mass hypnosis on a scale never possible in previous ages. These and many other things are symptoms of an overall situation. We have chosen—or been compelled against our free will—to live in "interesting times." What is around us has something to do with ourselves; if read correctly, the signs of catastrophe and destruction give us the clues as to why we are here and what we must do to find the antidote to them. They teach us about ourselves, imploring us to learn to live differently.

Facing the present world situation, a great many people know instinctively that they have to change from the way their predecessors lived, but are uncertain of how to go about this. The changes, they feel, need to occur both on an individual level (they cannot simply continue working for a higher income and material comfort) and on a global level (conventional ways of life lead to environmental and humanitarian degradation in the world). The turmoil of today leads to very interesting opportunities for those who consciously set out on their paths. Young people today have undreamed-of possibilities in the progress they can make. Many of them seem to have come to the Earth with great talents, qualities that are theirs by instinct and which members of an earlier generation had to struggle hard to acquire. But these young people are also subject to great forces of manipulation that shape their opinions and what they do. Who among them will have the stamina and courage to walk their own path and renounce the way of the herd?

The path changes as it is journeyed. We who travel together know that as soon as one of us masters one style of walking, the terrain will probably change so that we will need to find another. The compass for how to conduct oneself is within, and yet it is often other people who are the greatest sources of assistance. How you are doing on the path will be reflected in them. Certainly some of them will cause you grief; they may even tempt you to forsake your path, but without them the path is impossible. It is not easy to view with tolerance every person's wandering steps. Yet, other people are divine fragments around us, each connected to us in some mysterious way. Individuals go their own way, guided by obscure signs and symbols that they sometimes understand and sometimes misread and lose their way completely. People struggle as individuals toward their truth. We can all seem so very isolated, as if Truth has been separated into an infinite number of tiny fragments. As individuals, we must find our own designated piece of it for ourselves. When we do so, we also find Truth as a whole and gain a much greater understanding of what is at work in those other human beings.

Truth in its relation to individuals is something existential, something that lights up only when it has been *lived*. "There may well be Truth," says the seeker. "I, however, must find *my* truth." And if one does that, and if another is doing it at the same time and in close proximity, the two may not be aware of each other for a long time. Although there are times when we have companions, there are other times in which we are like people climbing a mountain in bad weather. Many are making the climb, but the way is blanketed with mist, and they are snow-blind and not able to see a single other soul. Only very rarely does a moment arise when the mist is blown away a little so that we see a shape in the distance and know we are not alone. The moment is fleeting and in no time the mist returns once more. This is the normal state of events upon the path, however the mountain does not go on forever and there will be a point reached when the mist and snow will end. The seeker will come to an entrance hall, and there she will see others, also filing in after their long time in the wilderness alone. They were in her vicinity all the time but are only now revealed.

As already said a number of times, the real guidance is within us, and anything anyone can say that is not the speech of our own souls must be taken with a grain of salt. Salt is a symbol in fairy tales for the powers of thought, and it is necessary for us to make use of our powers of thought. Through thinking we must digest, rework, and reconstitute everything that we receive and make it truly our own. You, the reader, are the only one who can solve the riddles of your own life. However, it is foolish to disregard the wisdom of others. Human progress is marked by signposts of others who have passed that way at different times. Many people have contributed insights that shine a light for those who want to find their own place in the ongoing drama of human history. We are not dumped into this world with no preparation; we are who we are through the accumulated experiences of many individuals.

The starting point in all discussion about who you are in relation to the world must be your own human soul. You are unique—and yet you are also the child of your times. Certain things have been happening that have had their affect on the consciousness of everyone around you. You share with others certain fundamental differences from people born in the Middle Ages, the Renaissance, or Ancient Greece. This kind of consciousness that you have inherited influences who you are. Let us take a look at this.

Human beings today, as in no other time in history, have an inner emptiness. This could be taken as a somewhat surprising statement, and I would expect some people to disagree with me, perhaps very strenuously. These are rich times; we travel to all parts of the world, create art and technology as never before, and experience life in vivid and meaningful ways. The past is open to us and we seem to be creating our own future. Surely people today are *full*, not empty. Yes, but the suicide rate has never been higher either. And who among us has not experienced times when our fullness felt more like a thin and vulnerable façade? Perhaps we have also faced the question: if that facade were to crumble, what would be found behind it? Twenty-first-century human beings in their souls are like those who live in an earthquake zone. The solid reality is actually far from solid—it is thin and sometimes it is as if one can feel the primordial forces just beneath one's feet. And every so often a small quake comes along, and the people wait, wondering, "Is *this* going to be the big one?"

Emptiness. As I said, we have not been dumped into the world without preparation, yet the prevailing soul mood of hundreds of thousands of our contemporaries sees a profound distance between themselves and others who have gone before. They suffer—*we* suffer—from inner emptiness, and this condition is so prevalent that it is easily accepted as the norm and barely noticed. Human beings in the past were not like this. Read William Golding's *The Inheritors*.[2] He gives a remarkable account of our human ancestors' consciousness. They lived at a level of consciousness that existed prior to the activity of thought as we know it; they had a kind of picture consciousness. In the past, we all lived our lives in such pictures, and the vivid immediacy of those received images was only gradually replaced by thoughts, which we have come to feel we create for ourselves. Through a gradual progression, the pictures and the feeling of connectedness with all life have been taken from us, and we are left with silence and emptiness. This silence is a most exciting phase. The most amazing symphonies ever written begin with silence. It is openness. But at this precise moment, it hangs heavily over many of us. Its suffering is spreading throughout many parts of the world. Emptiness. Silence. Separation. Somewhere in our memory we know that it was not always like this, and there is a yearning to break free into something different.

You must think this over for yourself. I haven't tried to gather up statistics to prove my hypothesis that humankind today suffers from a new kind of emptiness. I leave it to your own judgment and to your own observation of your experiences in life. It is my assertion that it is very important, as a starting point to treading the path, that one understands one's own particular kind of emptiness. The start of self-knowledge and the birth of wisdom lie in the acknowledgement of emptiness.

When emptiness is unacknowledged, all sorts of things can breed, attracted to the vacuum of ignorance. Hate breeds in the place where love could come into being if only a person's emptiness is acknowledged and worked with. Fear breeds where there is a longing for inner strength, doubt and despair where we have the greatest yearning for transcendent, radiant knowledge. However, when you own and recognize your emptiness, it can become fertile ground for insight. The beginning of liberation lies in what you *do* about it.

There are plenty of self-confident egoists today. Rock stars strut their stuff on the stage, politicians and televangelists speak passionately with fundamentalist certainty about how they are always right and will fix everything, always telling us that wrongs can be eliminated if you only buy the right product. But if we look at such self-confident people and what they are saying in a matter-of-fact way, it doesn't take much insight to recognize them as people desperate to hide their ignorance. Somehow during the last hundred or so years, word has gotten out that the emperor—you and I—has no clothes. In the nineteenth century, people did not know this, and they felt self-confident and believed in their place in history. Now we have come to see our fundamental nakedness in the depths of our souls. In the superficial parts of our being we can deny that this is so, but we cannot really fool ourselves; people today are uncomfortable with who they are. We are no longer able to project the confidence and fullness that define the nineteenth century.

When there is an acknowledged emptiness, what are we to do about it? When we are hungry or thirsty we try to get food or water. What if they are not available? We suffer. Perhaps, if we are thirsty, we accept a substitute that takes the thirst away for a while, even though it does not really satisfy. Perhaps there are those who wish to profit from our predicament and sell us cheap substitutes or even poison. When we have taken this in and realized it is only covering up our thirst for a time and not satisfying it, then we must try and get that poison out of our system and look for the real thing. Days of longing are before us. Even when we have the good fortune to find a gushing spring, we cannot be sure it will be there tomorrow. This is the situation we all face. Men and women of the twenty-first century have emptiness within them. They hope it will be filled, but even the wisest and most self-confident people have no way to guarantee that it will.

When you understand and accept your emptiness and when you have found out that it is not fatal and that it can be endured, you will be less driven to take in any old liquid that is at hand. You can start to discriminate and learn how to access what your body and soul really need. You will probably be unable to satisfy yourself completely. To be alive in our time is to be aware always of the zone of emptiness and lack of inner fulfillment. Real nourishment, real refreshment, comes from springs upon which we have no claim of ownership. Grace is something that is not given as a matter of course. We are beggars of the spirit. This is our starting point for understanding the contemporary human being and for understanding ourselves.

This is the first of the seven chapters I am writing to you about the path and the inner life of people today. It is simply a starting point. All we have achieved so far—if we have achieved anything—is to acknowledge together that we do not know everything. From this promising beginning, we shall go further.

SUMMARY OF CHAPTER 1: THE STARTING POINT

The turmoil in the world today is a clue that human beings need to learn how to live differently from how their predecessors have lived. People today live their own lives, struggling toward their truth as if Truth itself has been divided into many fragments. Yet Truth does exist and can be found through many different existential paths.

The starting point for any inquiry must be the human soul. The unique consciousness of our times is defined by the fact that we each experience a certain quality of emptiness in our life— the connectedness that people formerly possessed has been taken away from us. Silence and emptiness as a prelude for great things to come. The need for each person to understand one's own particular kind of emptiness. Emptiness unacknowledged can be the breeding-ground for evil but emptiness acknowledged is a first step toward freedom. That we are "beggars of the spirit"—that "real nourishment, real refreshment, comes from springs upon which we have no claim of ownership."

2

What Is Happening in the Soul?

"Caminante, no hay camino, se hace camino al andar."
(*Walker, there is no path. The path is made by walking.*)

—Antonio Machado[1]
"It goes slower these days, but it comes from a deeper place."
—Beethoven[2]

In earlier centuries there have always been a few pioneers who trod their own paths in a way that would become general to all people in later times. There are many examples—I mentioned one of these already, the fifteenth-century initiate Christian Rosenkreutz. Another is the knight Parsifal, a legendary figure but based on someone who really existed. In the ninth century it was Parsifal's destiny to go through hardships that were a kind of foreshadowing of the trials and tribulations many contemporary people inwardly encounter on a regular basis today. He had to endure a particularly acute form of what I called "emptiness" in the last chapter but which I could also call "alienation." The consciousness of others at that time, secure in the cocoon of beliefs they were born with, was vastly different from his. The average citizen of the time simply did not know the kind of loneliness and separation from meaning that became the defining feature of Parsifal's life. Parsifal drank deeply from this cup of loneliness

9

and was guided to find a way to break through it. His life can be an inspiration to people of our time.[3]

Another interesting figure who relates also to this theme was the sixteenth-century monk, St. John of the Cross.[4] He described a path of drawing closer to God through spiritual exercise, prayer, and devotion. It was not an easy process, for the one who trod it went through periods of intense self-doubt, anxiety, and loneliness that actually intensified as God drew closer. John called these periods "the dark night of the soul" and "the dark night of the spirit." He articulated what those who trod "the path made by walking" went through in his time, but what he wrote is full of relevance also to present-day spiritual seekers.

In the twentieth century, revolutions took place not only in the outer world but also in people's inner lives. It became more and more necessary to leave behind, at least to some degree, the secure social forms that had served people for generations and to work instead out of one's own inner compass. Individuals had done this before in previous centuries, but to have it happening almost as a mainstream event was something completely new. Before the twentieth century people were protected to a very great extent by social forms, habits, and conventions. Your world might be ripped apart in an earthquake or a war, someone close to you might die, but, by and large, the inner structure of society would reassert itself and, as you healed physically and emotionally, you would not face an inner abyss.

The twentieth century was a time of transition. Alongside many great innovations in how to live, we can easily observe how frantically some have attempted to hold on to anything that will delay the need to face the emerging imperative of the times. What is that imperative? It is the requirement to create out of nothing the social forms that do not yet exist. It is an inconvenient necessity and most people will do everything they can to avoid having to undertake such revolutionary (or shall we say evolutionary) inner struggle. Nevertheless, the times move inexorably and this work becomes increasingly necessary for our soul and spiritual health.

Throughout the twentieth century many social forms were being dismantled. Now, in another century, a very great number of those forms that sustained us in the past are gone. Yes, banks continue to function, people continue to live and work, marry and raise families, but all is totally different now. Society—in the sense of the social forms that we inherit—is in a fundamental sense hollow to many people today, hollow and meaningless. For these individuals, living on the cusp of two ways of life, fate has decreed that they encounter the emptiness of the world into which they have been born. Simultaneously they experience a most wonderful challenge and sense of freedom and a most complete and terrifying absence of meaning and of hope. Not everyone in the Western world encounters such a situation or can admit that it is happening, but it is the underlying inner drama that many people experience in life.

There was no exact point at which the transition from fullness to emptiness took place, but one moment in which many people began to see more clearly was during the First World War. This was a war created by the world's capitalist rulers, hidden in the usual appeals to patriotism and "God on our side," which politicians always use. Those who were fighting in the trenches experienced with particular intensity the gap between what they were being told by their leaders and the physical reality of trench warfare. One who experienced this—not directly as a soldier but through intuitive understanding and by way of her intense connection with a brother who was killed—was the New Zealand writer Katherine Mansfield. She expressed these thoughts in letters to her husband. In November 1919, a year after the war had ended, she was reviewing a new novel by Virginia Wolf and had the impression that the writer was trying to pretend that the war had never been and had thus written a book that is "a lie in the soul." Mansfield went on:

> It is really fearful to see the "settling down" of human beings. I feel in the profoundest sense that nothing can ever be the same—that, as artists, we are traitors if we feel otherwise; we have to take it into account and find new expressions, new thoughts, and feelings....
>
> I can only think in terms like "a change of heart." I can't imagine how after the war these men can pick up the old threads as though it had never been. Speaking to you, I'd say we have died and live again. How can that be the same life? It doesn't mean that life is the less precious or that 'the common things of light and day' are gone. They are not gone; they are intensified; they are illumined. Now we know ourselves for what we are. In a way it's a tragic knowledge: it's as though, even while we live again, we face death. But through Life, that's the point. We see death in life as we see death in a flower that is fresh unfolded. Our hymn is to the flower's beauty; we should make that beauty immortal because we know.[5]

Because we know. She hadn't fought herself, but the war had come close to her and been absorbed by her, and nothing could be the same for her again.

We who have been born after Katherine Mansfield are in many ways her children. We certainly know a great number of people who live as if events such as wars had never been, and if we are honest we can probably identify that tendency also within our-selves. It's not entirely a bad thing to forget the past, and to be able to make the most of the present is a necessary part of human nature—a testimony to human resilience. However, there is a fine line between this and escapism, the deliberate forgetfulness of who we really are and the self-chosen tasks for which we have come to Earth. "We died and live again. How can that be the same life?" People today may take drugs or plug music into their ears, but everyone today knows at some level that they are a part of all the suffering life of our time. Consciously or subconsciously we are all aware of the "inconvenient truths" that it would be much more comfortable not to know. In Mansfield's time only the most courageous of people were prepared to integrate these truths into their daily lives following the war. Katherine Mansfield was one of these and was horrified by the postwar attitudes of those who wished only to return to a way of life whose day was past and should never return.

Something similar is revealed in *An Inspector Calls*,[6] J. B. Priestley's prophetic play set before World War I but written in 1945. In the play a catastrophic revelation of the true state of affairs within a family takes place and is witnessed by all the members of that family. The older ones think it can be ignored and that life will return to being as it was. Mansfield knew that people who felt this way were essentially trying to put themselves back to sleep. She herself had been awakened and could not go back to the past, could not allow herself to be lulled into the half-sleeping life of an automaton.

What Mansfield wrote in those sentences quoted is a deep cry of protest as she sees others devoting the best powers of their lives to papering over the cracks that had opened up in the conventional world and pretending all was as it should be. This, she could not do. Do we not meet the attitude of avoidance everywhere in our time? Whole industries are devoted to it. If we wake we will pay a price for our awareness. But by studying the times we shall see that there is also a price for not waking, and that price, as Priestley's Inspector Goole tells us, is likely to be a bloody one. We *must* awake!

If we do awake and remain awake, doom and gloom is not the result of our new sense of connection with life and the intensification of feelings we all experience. If we can embrace the new consciousness of this age, we feel joy and sorrow simultaneously and find that we must search continuously for the "new expressions, new thoughts, and new feelings" that are appropriate to this new awareness. What we feel is still very new, and we are uncertain and will probably suffer many lapses into the old consciousness—acting as if our life is separate from others—before the twenty-first century has run its course. But if we are true to our heart's voice, we will realize there is no going back.

As well as being a very blood-soaked era, the twentieth century was a period when it was possible, as never before, for human beings to confront the world with a certain degree of honesty. A few very great individuals of that time, in finding their own roadmaps, produced new forms suitable for maps to serve the needs of many others. From among many, I have chosen Erich Fromm's classic, *To Have or to Be?*[7] Writing some forty years ago, he provides insight into the totalitarian techniques of mass deception and how an individual can resist them—insights that are as relevant today as they were then. He is only one example. Excellent map-makers have passed on their grasp of the situation as it dawned in them. We do not have to follow the herd and live as the puppet-masters would have us live. Great souls from the past gave their lives so that we might have insight into what is going on. They would wish us to involve ourselves in what they achieved, and if we are open to this we stand on their shoulders. Our personal drama is similar to theirs, regardless of whether we wish to take up our path and be authentic children of our time or surrender to the "avoidance industry" and "weapons of mass distraction."

There were many losses in the course of the twentieth century. The victories tend to be smaller, individual ones—"soul size" as Christopher Fry put it. The insight of Erich Fromm, the courageous inner pilgrimage and mapmaking of Carl Jung, the out-streaming of the holiness in action of Mahatma Gandhi or Mother Teresa, Rudolf Steiner's fundamental breakthrough in spiritual insight and his ability to communicate it, Dag Hammarskjöld, Martin Luther King Jr., and John F. Kennedy working from powerful will amid the greatest evils—all these are major victories achieved first on the *inner* plane. These individuals all began their journey in the spirit of Thomas Huxley's words: "Every great advance in natural knowledge has involved the absolute rejection of authority."[8] By rejecting outer norms and finding their own inner authority, the individuals mentioned here successfully navigated the questions of their own lives and were able to offer their knowledge, guidance, and inspiration to those who would come later.

Have people not somehow become smaller in recent times? We don't see a Mahatma Gandhi or a Dag Hammarskjöld in any visible place of authority today. These people in their time were able to shine. They gave something of themselves to those who came later. In a sense they disappeared into those who came after them. The "great ones" of our time are less conspicuous—they do less out of their own genius and yet the genii of some of the great teachers of the twentieth century are working through them. It is not the time to look for supermen; ordinary people must do the tasks the supermen did not complete. The great tasks of today need to be picked up by individuals who hear an inner call to fulfill them. These individuals will act alone; though they may be in partnership with others, there will be no one who can tell them what they should do and no one there to lean on for support.

The tasks today are great; the puppet-masters would have us go on a path that ends in terrible, gray slavery. The fate of humanity is in the hands of those who are aware of this. Edward Snowden is an example today of a young person who, with no pretensions, saw what he had to do and acted out of his own convictions, even at the cost of his own life. The loneliness that such individuals encounter in their times of great decision is depicted in the 2015 Oscar-winning documentary, *Citizen Four*. In it, we witness the moment when Snowden has to cut the threads to his previous life and, knowing he cannot go back, faces up to the great unknown ahead of him. We can imagine other such heroes and potential heroes everywhere around the world. If you are prepared to live your life authentically and follow your own path, you cannot be certain where it will lead you.

Are there more young people today equipped to handle the situation they have been born into? Can they bear the naked reality in all its godforsaken emptiness as it gradually dawned in human beings during the course of the twentieth century? Many strategies for avoiding the truth have been dismantled in recent years. Of course, new sources of distraction continually appear. Freedom to choose is always present—the choice to tread one's path or to avoid it. There is a void today in which the old social forms have disappeared. Nature (including human nature) hates a vacuum and will always fill it with something if she can. If the substance that fills the void is not created out of the individual's own will, a negative substance, born of fear and emptiness, will find its way into the soul instead. This is how two particular forces take root in the soul: *addiction* and *fundamentalism*. The two are related, because each is a reaction to the emptiness that all human beings who are open to our time endure. Addiction manifests when people try to fill their inner emptiness without realizing that the chosen substance actually works in a way contrary to what the user desires. Fundamentalism is the result of an attempt to fill a void of fear and emptiness with false and deceptive certainty. Let us look at these two qualities in turn.

ADDICTION

One can be addicted to many different things. Food, sex, narcotics, and the like, of course, but there are also more subtle forms of addiction, such as a need always to live in comfort or to be recognized by others. We can be addicted to a person (a common phenomenon that, in its early stages, is sometimes called *being in love*) or indulge in addictive behaviors. Addiction is often hidden but it is something very common, so common that we can justifiably ask: are there any individuals at all who are *not* addicted to something?

Anything that goes beyond the basic processes of maintaining the physical body can become an addiction. Our feeling of emptiness—always lurking, usually unacknowledged—is the root cause that allows all problems of addiction to come into existence. We demand a certain soul-stimulation, and if we don't get it we experience disappointment and frustration. If we do get what we are after, our emptiness is concealed for a time by the satisfaction of the desire. However this satisfaction lasts only a short time, whereas the sense of emptiness is something that endures. It is there in the souls of people today as a kind of constant background—an inner blues accompaniment that can be heard even when the dancers in the foreground have the volume turned right up. Some people have the capacity to endure it, to go beyond it, and to find out what it is concealing, but many do not, especially as the emptiness that they feel is unacknowledged by them or seen as something weak or shameful. Very quickly they can be led by one of the many practices of avoidance technology toward a dance of desire/satisfaction/desire that is the exact opposite of the spiritual path. The spiritual path has periods of testing and of suffering, but there are also times of confirmation in which you know you are growing and developing and becoming more fully yourself. That opposite kind of path—one of Shakespeare's characters calls it the "primrose path"[9]—leaves a person feeling more and more alienated from life, more and more empty and less and less able to deal with that emptiness. "Rock bottom" is the state where you feel you can't go any further down and you resolve to change, but many people never get to that point. They simply go on their dance of desire-emptiness-desire ("the dance of the *dead*") and justify it to themselves with the conviction that this is just the way life is—that this is "human nature."[10] It may be quite some time before they realize that they have not reached their desired human potential.

Young people are targets for addiction because they experience with particular intensity the anguish of their emptiness. It will be well for them to understand that this emptiness is not something they can run away from. If they try to deaden it with an addictive substance or addictive patterns of behavior it may seem to be restrained for a time but will actually grow and demand to be faced at a later date when it is even more powerful.

Addiction is a doomed attempt to remove the ever-constant threat of inner emptiness. Addicts are searching for a means to ease the pain they feel continually within their hearts. Anything that the soul takes in passively to hide an emptiness or to numb a pain may become the soul's object of addiction. However, are there ways to transcend such emptiness that are *not* addictive?

Although many behaviors may result from trying to fill emptiness, there is really only one way that carries no danger and that can be assured of success—*the way of inner activity*. Those suffering the anguish of alienation from the culture of the heart must generate meaning by engaging their own creativity. Inner restlessness and the search for distraction is addictive, but a true, self-created activity that brings one more strongly into life is not. Individuals determine their own activity. There will be as many forms of inner activity as there are persons creating them, but in each of these the soul will not be passively led. Inner creativity will be born as a form of full participation in surrounding life. Participation, entering life fully with one's whole being, is what people today long for. The opposite of being a participant in life is to become the kind of person that advertisers and our totalitarian rulers want us to become: passive consumers. Everywhere in our time we meet the forces that attempt to turn us into inactive spectators and passive consumers. Not to be dumbed down is to resist these forces with inner power of will.

In this century, doing what is right in one's own life has nothing to do with fulfilling abstract standards. The good action—that which enters fully into life and brings an answering confirmation back—begins at the very place where you are standing now. We need to ask ourselves: *What, in fact, is the loneliness or dissatisfaction that I feel?* We should not try to answer this question immediately, but rather experience it as clearly and as fully as possible. When it has been experienced intensively enough, we can begin to search for the thoughts and actions that will carry us across the bridge of alienation and into the state of participation and fulfillment. Stand first within the nothingness. Do not look for a quick fix. Only when you have tasted the atmosphere of the void with enough intensity can answers start to arise from out of it. Only when you have lived through your nothingness fully enough can you begin to create its antidote. Because this is taking place in your own inner being, you are the only one who can heal it. Books may help, people may give support, but the solution of the great problems will be in learning to be spiritually active for yourself.

Herman Hesse's novel *Steppenwolf*,[11] quoted at the start of chapter 1, describes wonderfully a man experiencing this alienated state of soul, awareness of suffering the constant wound of unfulfillment. The wound is never entirely healed in the novel, but the predicament of one suffering person before he has attained his own creative solution is shown with intensity and truth. Although it is about a man in his late forties and although it was written many decades ago when the author was close to sixty years of age, it is a powerful statement of the problems of our time experienced by youth. As Hesse himself relates, it tended to be understood only partially by the readers of his day. They saw the wounded state of Steppenwolf's soul and many identified with this, but by and large they did not comprehend the vast springs of healing that Hesse believed existed and depicted in glimpses throughout the novel. Most readers are unable to understand the kind of activity that the Steppenwolf needs to experience to bring healing to himself and to the society with which he is at odds.

Steppenwolf experiences the void of nothingness within him intensely, but it was Hesse's belief that this alienation was a temporary condition that he had power to transcend. In the years since *Steppenwolf*, we have had thousands of novels that depict characters who suffer the various forms of the illness that Steppenwolf suffers, but few authors show the sources of healing or depict ways they can be accessed. Today it is as if we are all expected to believe that being on Earth is like living in a closed system into which nothing transcendental can gain access. This *Roadmap* is based on the conviction that earthly existence in not at all a closed system and that the answers to the questions we set for ourselves are at hand if we can learn how to ask these questions with sufficient energy, perseverance, and patience.

Today one hopes that young people can see both sides of the problem that Hesse depicted so vividly, that they are prepared to look truthfully into their own fractured and lonely inner nature, but that they can also trust that springs of healing are totally accessible to them. In other words, one hopes that we can all find the way to solve the problem of addiction for ourselves.

FUNDAMENTALISM

Fundamentalism, on the other hand, is less a matter of the heart than the head. It is the state of soul that arises when one takes what might be true and fixes it too soon into an absolute truth. Truth has to be *lived*, and that takes time. One of the temptations of life is that, as human beings, we are continually encouraged to save time and stand under a banner of something we have not really made our own. People fall for it all the time because we all deeply long for certainty and security. Addiction involves satisfying a desire that is not yet purified, a desire that has not yet been transformed into love. Fundamentalism consists of doing the same thing to an intellectual desire. In each case a genuine longing for fulfillment is satisfied too soon.

Fundamentalism is more common than we think. My bank manager is being a fundamentalist when he tells me he didn't know that the bank he works for holds $642 billion in assets and $2.9 trillion in speculative trade in derivatives,[12] and then tells me that he is not at all worried by this. He has a naïve faith in something that he has not thought through. Life is complex and such facts as the one above are not publicized (if they were it would be judged a scandal very quickly), but this illustrates how we are all fundamentalists to some extent, in that we tend to live with a naïve faith that things are all right without knowing the truth of what really lies below the surface. Emerging from fundamentalism, testing facts with an open mind, is uncomfortable but necessary for anyone who wishes to become a free human being.

Those who have succumbed to the temptation of premature gratification will be led in a direction that is the very opposite of where they really want to go. Resisting the temptations of certainty of thought and nonfulfillment of feeling, even when we are sorely pressed and in pain, is a great deed that needs to be renewed continually. The English poet John Keats called it "negative capability," the ability to forego quick solutions and to live, perhaps for years or decades, without security, knowing, or satisfaction. It is in this state that the truth may gradually ripen.[13] The seed must die before the new plant is born into the world and it takes courage to endure that death. There is always an element of fear when an individual dares to exercise negative capability. Many medical practitioners and fixers of all kinds will offer the sufferer quick solutions, chemical or otherwise, to cure the discomfort that is being felt. The pain of nonfulfillment is portrayed in the media as a great curse, but one that a person can easily remove by spending a few dollars.

What happens to the one who does not take the easy way out, who puts up with pain at "the boundary of the bearable"[14] and endures the anguish of negative capability? This takes us to the topic of our next chapter. The person who refuses to be satisfied with a premature solution approaches a kind of *threshold*. We must examine the nature of this threshold. What is it and how can it be crossed? It will be the theme of the next three chapters. But before going into it there in more detail, I would like to say the following:

Young people today are born to meet the challenges of crossing the threshold. They can do it. Of course, very little guidance and practical orientation can be offered in a book or by another person. We must all make the crossing on our own. But this is something we were born to do, and there is no reason why we cannot do it successfully. In contrast to previous generations, by being alive in the twenty-first century we have the good fortune to have what we need to make the crossing. Before moving on to consider what must be done, take a moment to feel this sense of confidence in yourself. If you can locate it now, if you can foster it and resolve to hold it firm during other times in your life, then you will have attained something of infinite importance for your future. You have within you everything needed to make the crossing. Yes, this is certainly true; the faculties by which you will succeed are already within you, not somewhere outside.

Be aware of how this thought resonates within you. If it seems correct (although we may not yet be clear about what we mean by "crossing the threshold"), then get used to feeling its presence and how this can be renewed in many and various moments of one's life. You are powerful. You can know fulfillment without falling into the aberrations of fundamentalism or addiction, ignorance, or despair. You can, you *will*, become free.

SUMMARY OF CHAPTER 2: WHAT IS HAPPENING IN THE SOUL?

The "path made by walking" as something that cannot be avoided today. Pioneers of it from the past. How antiquated social forms have broken down in our time so that there is a universal need to "create out of nothing the new social forms that do not yet exist." Katherine Mansfield as a progenitor of one who came to understand the new reality after World War I. There are whole industries devoted to avoidance, and people are desperate to lull themselves to sleep. However, there is no going back to the past for people today. The new consciousness of the age, though hard to bear, also brings great joy. Some twentieth-century individuals embraced the new consciousness and produced their own "road-maps" that are available to seekers today. The great ones of the past have had their life-tasks divided up among many today. In our times it is necessary to find one's true tasks because simply doing what one is told takes the world into a terrible slavery. Edward Snowden is an example of a contemporary person who was prepared to sacrifice for his beliefs.

When people cannot endure emptiness, something alien to their individuality enters their soul life to fill the vacuum there; addiction and fundamentalism arise in this way. Addiction is an attempt to find an easy solution to heal the pain of emptiness in the heart. Against this, as a true healing of the wounds of the heart, stands creativity—the way of inner activity, which is the opposite of inner restlessness and the search for distraction. "Inner restlessness and the search for distraction is addictive, but a true, self-created activity that brings one more strongly into life is not. Individuals determine their own activity." Steppenwolf—his illness and the sources of healing for the alienation that he experiences. And fundamentalism is what arises when a person tries to heal prematurely the wound of emptiness not so much in the heart as in the head.

Negative capability as the ability to resist the temptations of premature gratification. When this is practiced a person approaches a kind of threshold. This threshold—what it is and how we can cross it—will be the theme of the next three chapters. Final words of encouragement that you have been born to make this crossing in your own individual way and that you have within you what you need to achieve this.

3

The Nature of the Threshold

"It is time for you to stop talking about the Holy Spirit and to start to talk out of the Holy Spirit."

(attributed to the anonymous fourteenth-century layperson who became Johannes Tauler's spiritual teacher [1])

The previous chapter said that to live in the state of inner emptiness—resisting the temptation to surrender to fundamentalism or addiction—is to live in a kind of borderland where we approach a threshold. The word *threshold* does not mean outer barrier; the threshold exists for all human beings, and the psychic health of our human nature depends on how some of us make the crossing. This chapter is concerned with providing a fuller picture of what is meant by *threshold* and how it manifests to people today, especially the young.

What is a human being? I could employ the language of reductive science and say I am 65 percent oxygen, 18.5 percent carbon, and so on, but I will approach the question in a better way through a metaphor. In Hesse's words in *Steppenwolf,* we are a "narrow and perilous bridge between nature and spirit."[2] The river over which the bridge is suspended and all the air above is in the realm of the borderland. When we are moving toward the side of the river called "spirit," we are in this borderland and encounter the threshold. As we approach the shore, the resistance of the threshold becomes stronger. The threshold, if we cross it, takes us through into the spiritual world. This does not mean necessarily that we see angels; rather, it might simply mean an awareness of existing for a while within a web of self-sustained spiritual thought. In our thinking, we regularly move between the two shores of the river, between nature and spirit. If our questions here are predominantly about quantity, then proximity to the natural side of the shore is perfectly valid. However, if the questions are more qualitative, then we need to move immediately away from that side of the shore and approach the side where the threshold awaits.

When we consider a qualitative question, our thoughts frequently lack the inner force to go beyond a certain point on the bridge. The crossing is incomplete, and we find ourselves banished from the region of the threshold back into the borderland. The threshold, as we approach it, can be compared to a high region on Earth where the air is thin. When we experience oxygen deprivation, we become faint and may collapse or be forced to turn back. We cannot continue unless we manage to take in more oxygen, by having developed our lungs to a greater capacity than normal or by using an artificial breathing apparatus. In the region of the threshold, our thoughts experience a similar deprivation of what they need to sustain them. With no artificial apparatus, we have to become more powerful in our ability to remain connected to the seed of living thinking within us. Our dead, intellectual thoughts are left behind as we approach the threshold, but we carry within us a way of relating to the world that can live in the rarified air of that region—if it can become strong enough to survive the crossing.

If we were to give up every attempt to cross, discouraged and exhausted by the constant rebuttal to our efforts, we would be forced to retreat to the other side of the bridge and curl up between the rocks of a stagnant pool like an old crayfish. We would become earth-bound and reactive creatures, frozen and immobile, endlessly repeating the meaningless rituals of earthly existence, and convinced we are right. We probably all know people who have become like that. However, such a retreat is actually difficult to sustain, because distorted messages from the other side continue to reach us and disturb our dreams. Those scrambled signals of another reality maintain what is human in us and prevent us from lying down in the rocks where we have fallen. We are goaded back to the bridge, compelled to trudge always somewhere upon the narrow, perilous place of our humanity—the bridge that spans the borderland. This is our lot until we learn how to strengthen our power of thought and consistently negotiate the threshold. It is the experience of Sisyphus, the day-to-day human condition.

The borderland is where we are during just about every waking moment of our lives. In the borderland, our proximity to the threshold will vary—sometimes we are closer, and sometimes farther. The threshold itself is not some kind of solid wall; rather, it is a dynamic force that responds to our own energies, something that moves with us and against us, becoming stronger when we start to approach the "spirit" side of the river—when we are closer to true *qualitative thinking*.

What is thought? Thinking receives bad press, because when we think we are "in our head," which is considered inferior to being in our heart or limbs. There are undoubtedly numerous examples of useless, abstract thinking without which the world would be better off, and worse, even dangerous and malevolent fabrications. However, the quality of thought that takes place in purity across the threshold—thinking that people hundreds of years ago considered to originate with the Holy Spirit—deserves to be regarded as entirely different from our plodding, earthbound intellectuality or the poisonous activity of destruction. Thinking that is not shadowy, intellectual, and lifeless has the qualities of heart and will. Part of the task of this *roadmap* is to show how the heart and will can connect with our thinking.

It is the brain that acts as a receptor for thinking, and in recognition of this necessity for a person to possess a brain in order to think, some scientists promote the idea that the brain is responsible for the thoughts created. The brain, by this reasoning, is not unlike an orange juicer, squeezing out thoughts. This may be true of some thoughts; I can imagine thoughts that premeditate a murder being like this, squeezed out of a darkened soul with a grim focus on causing harm. I can picture a person being driven to act on inner compulsions, the brain squeezing out plots, step by step, and the actions needed to gratify inner urges. However, for the kinds of thoughts that we are interested in the brain is merely the medium through which thought is able to manifest. These thoughts involve heart and will and the thinker is sincerely trying to follow a path of thought with the fewest possible personal preconceptions.

When we hear a radio, we do not believe that the broadcast is somehow being extracted from the radio, but that the radio is a transmitter and that the program is broadcast elsewhere *through* the radio. Thoughts, too, come from somewhere else. Our brain is as essential in their apprehension as a radio is to picking up a radio station, but the brain does not create the thoughts any more than a radio creates what is being broadcast through it. If a radio is damaged it is possible to repair it. That this does indeed happen in life is revealed through brain research and observations that new neuron pathways can be created in the case of brain injury. This gives rise to the image of the "brain that heals itself." One fairly obvious question arises from this: No one talks of a "radio that heals itself," so why should that ability be attributed to the brain? Who or what creates new neuron pathways in the brain?

In the final sentence of Charles Darwin's *Origin of Species*, he spoke of "life with its several powers, having been originally breathed by the Creator into a few forms or into one."[3] He wanted to show that his evolutionary ideas provided a mechanism for the development of organisms on Earth, but that these ideas did not at all necessitate that life itself began in a mechanistic or godless way. God, a spirit, a creative power—something that provided the creative impetus of a beginning—breathed life into matter. That was all that Darwin, as a scientist, felt entitled to say. He later removed the reference to God altogether, restricting what he said in later editions of the *Origin* to, "life...having been breathed into a few forms..." Both statements still carry his conviction that it was outside his sphere of responsibility to speculate on the "first cause" of life, but that his work was related to discovering a mechanism ("secondary cause") for the subsequent development of living forms. To Darwin, the important thing was that we attended to the Earth we experience with our senses and intellect and that we study this to find the origin of life. This is a scientific approach, whereas beliefs and the words in holy books are not. Thus he offered the picture of human beings evolving physically on Earth, organisms developing gradually into increasingly com-plex forms.

It goes beyond the evidence to assert from this that we are the direct descendants of apes. What can be shown through the study of species is that a line of connection passes in a very exact and lawful fashion through all the kingdoms of the Earth. We share ancestors in common with apes—in fact we share ancestors with every living thing upon the Earth. But the spirit that breathed life into earthly dust left upon us three particular marks by which our divine origin is visible. These three signs are our capacities for thought, language, and upright stance. The second and third of these will be dealt with in the final two chapters; the one that needs to be approached first is our faculty for having thoughts. The realm of thinking is the realm in which we come closest to the spirit that set life into motion. If we cultivate the spark of thinking, we have the possibility not only of tracing our evolutionary journey as Darwin would see it, but of learning the language of our non-earthly origin.

We live at a time when we are challenged to do exactly this. Tracing the language of our spiritual origin is sometimes called being able to "read the Book of Nature" or "hear the Cosmic Word." To be sure, most of us do it but very slightly, but it is the new evolutionary challenge that is now before us—that we come to learn spiritual thinking and produce the kind of thought that brings us real tidings about what is spiritual within ourselves.

Yes, the faculty in which our divine origin is most closely reflected is the faculty of thinking, but not all kinds of thinking bring us close to the divine. We encounter the threshold when we think—but it is the *kind* of thinking that we employ which determines how strongly we shall rub up against this threshold and what sort of resistance we shall generate. If we sit back and watch DVDs or read comics in the sun and eat sausages all day we may never encounter it at all.

Our picture of borderland and threshold is a metaphor, but a living metaphor can be more fruitful than dry, abstract thoughts because a metaphor reminds us of the way all things are linked. We shall therefore continue to employ the metaphor of the threshold. It is, first of all, a gap between two regions. The really important question now is to ask: How can we cross the threshold? This crossing takes place when we think truthfully and with sufficient power. To understand the activity of crossing the threshold we need to look more closely at human thought.

Certain things in life are obvious—throw a stone up into the air and it will eventually fall back. Given the necessary information about the mass of the stone, its angle to the earth, its speed, air resistance, and the strength of the wind, we can work out where it will land simply by applying mathematical processes and thinking through all relevant thoughts. This is possible because the problem depends on nothing other than physical data—for example, weight, speed at impact, and angle to the earth. With other problems in which the data is not only to do with physical measurement, one simply does not have this kind of certainty. "If I decide to train as a chef, will that be good for my future?" There are facts in that question that *can* be drawn from the material world, but much more that cannot. It is an existential question—something one must work through over a period of time, something that has to be *lived*. Whenever we attempt to grapple with questions of this nature we must put up with a good deal of uncertainty. We agree to bear such uncertainty because we know we are on a path to finding the answer. A few months or years of being a chef will tell us if it was a good decision to do that training. If we discover it was a mistake, we will change course and do something different.

In general, we have a certain amount of self-knowledge and, apart from periods of crisis when our self-confidence may encounter a few well-needed knocks, we tend to feel we have the capacity to answer our own self-imposed questions about how to shape our lives. It is another matter when we start to consider questions involving more than ourselves. Questions involving other people and the society in which they live will have a quantifiable element to them, but there will be many other factors to be taken into account that are not at all quantifiable. What will our basis be for judgment on these inquiries? Scientific fact, perhaps? Individual rights? Human progress? The ecological wellbeing of the planet?

Our own feelings of knowing what we want will not be enough to guide us. Unless we choose to view all other human beings as identical to ourselves—something that experience will soon correct—we must admit that we face many unknowns.

Questions about the nature of our life and community demand much more than strict, fact-based logic. Yet these questions on a million topics as varied as peace, justice, the soul, the spirit, how to live one's life, and so on are undoubtedly some of the most important aspects of our experience. Most of us are prepared to grapple with them and believe that we can (perhaps in the company of others) pursue a path toward their solution. But answers are always hard-won—never easy.

We may reach a point with regard to some inquiries when we realize we lack a satisfactory basis to solve that matter without actual spiritual insight. How, for instance does a person faced with a certain set of circumstances decide the rights and wrongs of an abortion? We can refuse to think and base our decision solely on a preconceived "fundamentalist" view, whether "pro-life" (that abortion in all circumstances is a crime against life and is wrong) or "pro-choice" (that the mother in all circumstances has the right to choose what takes place in her own body). If we try and negotiate the spectrum between these two extremes and consider the situation from as many perspectives as possible, are we not forced to consider spiritual questions amid the facts? A child, when born, has human rights that few would deny. Do these rights start at birth or earlier? Where is the child during the nine months of pregnancy? To get a full picture, not just an Earth-centric one, we experience the need for objective insight into pre-earthly existence. But here we come up against a threshold; questions about the soul's immortality cannot be answered by the same methods we use to analyze the composition of matter.

A confirmed materialist would never consider such questions necessary but would consider the growth of the fetus in the mother's womb to be sufficient information to place beside the specific individual circumstances of the particular case. A spiritual view, on the other hand, would consider it imperative to know as much as possible about how a human soul gradually unites with its future physical body during the nine months of pregnancy. What is the experience of the incarnating soul during that time? What does that soul experience if the pregnancy is interrupted, whether by accident (miscarriage) or by active intervention (abortion)? What is the karma of such an intervention to all concerned—doctor, mother, and incarnating soul?

Many will say that no such information can be acquired and that we must base our decision on earthly facts alone. Too often such Earth-oriented thinking does not go beyond the stubborn assertion, "I don't know anything about that and no one else can know it either!" Since the start of the twentieth century, however, sources of knowledge have been available in the world that unite clear thinking within the physical conditions of the world with spiritual insight that can be seen by those who have more than earthly organs of perception. Most of what such people have said cannot be accepted yet by mainstream thinking, but those who are convinced that there *is* a spiritual reality cannot wait for mainstream thinking to change; for them it is more important to know how to be sure that the spiritual information they receive is true.

Once religious faith alone could substitute for our own thinking, but for a growing number of people today that is not enough; ideas must be carried by individual judgment, which must be supported by as much insight as possible, and such insight needs to be augmented by a spiritual view of the wholeness of life. If one is not completely hypnotized by materialism, this will be seen as an absolute necessity.

Those who need an answer to such a question and are prepared also to consider the big picture of an overarching spiritual reality over human life are on that bridge over the river and suspended above the abyss. No one likes to remain there for long; it is very uncomfortable. The more that our questions deal with matters beyond the merely quantifiable, the more it will seem to us that we are in a void and have lost the solid ground beneath our feet. The dogs of surrender are snapping at our heals, encouraging us to give up our quest for truth and settle for the easy options of fundamentalists or addiction. If we refuse to give in, we face assaults on our capacity for human integrity.

I am going to borrow an expression from the great twentieth century spiritual researcher and teacher Rudolf Steiner and call this region of uncertainty the *belt of lies*. We are still in the realm of metaphor, and the belt of lies is not a particular geographical region of the Earth any more than the threshold is somewhere you can drive up to in your car. Yet, like the threshold, the belt of lies does exist and we should become familiar with what it is like in order to survive it. It is a borderland area located between the place where the Earth gives stability in good quantitative answers and common sense and the place where answers are found to questions relating to an eternal reality. It is a place of great tension, and twenty-first-century people spend more time there than those of any other century. Our whole culture is surrounded by lies; industries are devoted to their continuation, and we can almost say our lives are cut from the fabric of the lie itself. This is not entirely a bad thing, since it presents us with the need for great activity. The results we bring back from the belt of lies can be significant if we accept the challenges and learn to make it our business to penetrate this region with our humanity and carry our awareness of it with us in our quest for truth.

The belt of lies is yet another name for the region of the threshold. It is the borderland where all kinds of falsehood prevail. Whenever we enter the world of the non-quantifiable by weight and measure, we are open to error that cannot be verified by data alone. One way scientists have dealt with this in the past two hundred years has been to erect a barricade around everything that could lead to such falsehood and say that it is beyond the scope of their inquiry. It was the French philosopher Auguste Compte who first proposed a formula that, scientifically at least, would ground human beings firmly on this side of the threshold. The philosophy he created is *positivism*, which states that we cannot know or be positive about anything that cannot be weighed or measured. This way of thinking need not fear the threshold, because it never comes anywhere near it. Limiting itself to the quantifiable, physical world, the worldview of positivism is wholly physical in nature.

In the social sciences today, various methods have been developed that recognize the validity of much that is not quantifiable. It is understood that human beings do not behave as predictably as two kinds of salt dissolved in a test tube. Yet the world in which we live has been hugely infected by humanity's long-standing bias toward empiricism. Things that exist outside the boundary of what can be weighed and measured (there are a great number of them—truth, the soul, life, one's experience of the color yellow, sorrow, the scale of C minor) can be considered by scientists under certain conditions, but in the popular media and in most minds, such things are considered "subjective" and thus, by definition, less important than quantifiable data or phenomena. The color yellow poses no problem when considered as a kind of radiation with a wavelength of a certain frequency; as a human soul-experience about which specific qualities can be identified, it is to be treated with skepticism. Scientific thinking that trusts only its instruments and dismisses human feelings and intuitions holds humanity under a kind of a spell.

Scientific thinking that results from positivism can be called *reductionism,* because it reduces everything to the data it can handle. By reducing everything to constituent physical components, it approaches everything as if it were dead. When we project the results of such science on the world, a nightmare is unleashed. Take from human beings all of which you cannot be factually certain, and you take away life, soul, and spirit. Human beings have been greatly reduced; you have subtracted from them everything that stops them from being a corpse. When the results and discoveries of reductionist thinking are brought into the world, the whole world is in danger of being turned into a gigantic graveyard.

In our twenty-first-century world, we are well on our way to turning our world into a place of death. We are all familiar with the present concern over the many environmental problems reaching critical levels today. They have been growing for many years, and we must face the fact that our very survival as a species is threatened. To do this, it helps to step back and consider in each individual case the kind of thinking that gave rise to these problems. Behind each of them, we find a degree of reductionist thinking. Dead, materialistic thinking fills the world with corpses, because it treats the world as a morgue, with no feeling for *life.*

In our time, the kinds of thinking that deal only with death have come very far. Whole industries such as various military industrial complexes throughout the world are devoted to destruction. In more hidden ways, destruction has become a part of daily life much more than we are aware of. To see what we are dealing with, it may be valuable to take a particularly extreme example— the Large Hadron Collider located at the European Center for Nuclear Research. In a seventeen-mile-long tunnel beneath the French–Swiss border near Geneva, scientists are doing research that involves smashing proton beams into each other at rates of up to a billion collisions a second. This is achieved through incredibly strong magnets, one of which has a magnetic field 100,000 times greater than the Earth's magnetic field. Despite huge risks in playing with such phenomenal energies, scientists doing this research are already planning something still more powerful.

The vision at work in such a place involves stripping away aspects of life that should remain connected (the photon from the entire hydrogen atom) and carrying out acts of destruction (the collision of the particles and what results from this) with ever-greater force. Unable to value the quality of reverence that true knowledge of life requires, the researchers attempt to get to the ultimate sources of life by storming the gates of knowledge through wielding ever greater physical power. They look at life only mechanistically, but life itself exists on a higher level than do machines. Life will never be understood by pulling it apart and destroying it.

Although this is an extreme example, the Large Hadron Collider is nevertheless a true child of its time. It embodies the prevailing scientific belief that we can know life by having power over it. To exercise power and control is the goal of many today; we are expected to control our children and pets, unwanted life forms, and undesirable criminal elements. We look up to the strong person who controls others. But the *good* human being whose source of action is love relinquishes such power. Humanity's next evolutionary challenge is to develop faculties far removed from the ideals of the will to power and control.

Positivist, reductionist thinking does not carry us into the future, for it remains on this side of the threshold. It can attain certainty in its own greatly limited sphere, but when its results are projected onto the world, it kills whatever it touches. The thoughts that will bring salvation to the Earth are the kind that do not reduce the world into lifeless processes. They are the processes of *living thinking*—the kind of thinking that is done with the *heart*. The biologist Rupert Sheldrake, who gave us the theory of "morphic fields," said the following in an interview with Otto Scharmer: "I chose biology because I loved animals. But I soon realized that the kind of biology I learned involved killing everything and cutting it up. Ever since, I've been driven by the question: What would it take to develop a science that enhances life?"[4]

The danger is that on the road between thinking with head alone and thinking with the heart, human beings are extremely susceptible to error. Reductionism developed in the world for a good reason—as an attempt to give humanity certainty. If we are to find a new certainty that is open to a wider universe than the narrow one provided by reductionism, then we must see if there is a way in which we can learn to trust our human feelings and intuitions. We need a method whereby our soul can be trained objectively to be a kind of scientific instrument to be relied upon in what it experiences and in its judgments of those experiences.

Such "schooling" means walking the path and a period of apprenticeship in the region of the threshold, because the realm from which intuitive, heart thinking originates is beyond the borderland region of the belt of lies. Before we can come to certainty about anything that is worth knowing, the region of lies and illusions must be passed through. Complete security of truth can be won only by taking one's questions across the threshold and bringing the answers back from the other side.

Something in us needs to change if we are to make the crossing. Our thinking, which generally seems adequate for this world, needs to become stronger before it can take us over the threshold. At this evolutionary moment humanity is engaged in a life-and-death struggle of finding the way to do exactly this. We need to transcend reductionism without losing our certainty. There are two dangers: fear that would stop us from pressing on into the unknown, and the possibility of colossal error if we go forward and lose the solid ground that the sensory world provides. We need to think with the heart.

Is this possible? How do we learn to do this? The only way to learn to swim is to enter the water. It is the same with learning to do heart thinking. Deep, evolutionary processes are leading more and more people to think in a new way. People today are being thrown by life into the "pool" of the threshold; some drown, but many are indeed learning to swim.

The first thing is to realize that enduring the affliction of "not knowing" (enduring *negative capability,* as described in the previous chapter) is a requirement of heart thinking. In the belt of lies, all kinds of forces and ideas are trying to fly in under the radar of our awareness. It is easier to use reductionist thinking, whereby we know we are accurate within certain limits. However, reductionism itself is a lie, and those who have realized this know they cannot continue confining their experiences to a straight-jacket. They inevitably adopt a broader worldview, but illusions are everywhere.

The philosophy of the New Age is, in general, a somewhat perplexing mixture of truth and error. Those who oppose any movement at all away from the data-only view of life are aware of this and know how to make it sound as if some of the movement's more crazy ideas are all there is to it. It will be a hard task to get the good ideas of the New Age movement taken up as a science because of all the rubbish that washes in along with its nuggets of gold. Avoiding error means rejecting solutions to our questions too quickly and learning to live with negative capability. People who get a sense for the direction of the future often lack patience and discrimination and are unprepared to go through the whole process needed to give them certainty and the ability to communicate their ideas effectively to others. The situation is similar to that in *The Chymical Wedding*. Christian Rosenkreutz, who walked the slow, direct path, guided truly by his inner compass, attends a marriage feast, at which many of the guests had arrived by clambering over all sorts of obstacles and forcing their away through, regardless of whether they had been invited.

To the nineteenth-century exponents of materialism, the situation we are encountering in our questioning would seem a nightmare. Those people needed their dependable, solid ground. But solidity is being taken away from us. From a high point of pure materialism in the late nineteenth century, human beings have been changing. Since the twentieth century, a large part of our science has dealt less with matter *per se* than with various ideas *about* matter. Scientists have taken up numerous hypotheses having to do with light waves, genes, atoms, molecules, and so on, and because of the human desire for fundamentalist certainty, they have begun to treat these ideas *as if they are facts*. Theories and concepts have been made literal; science has created a transcendental reality, forgetting that it is only a model, and projected it out into the world. Thus, adherents of materialism are increasingly distancing themselves from this world. Their worldview can be seen as a kind of "super-materialism," whereby thought forms that bear the stamp of the physical world actually go deeper than matter itself into the theoretically conceived powers of discrimination of the subearthly world. The practical consequences of inventions resulting from this kind of thinking reveal ever-greater powers of destruction.

Heart thinking is a requirement of our times—it is a new form of thinking that is gradually evolving through the heart working in partnership with the head. When head and heart are joined, the heart becomes objective through the discipline of thought. Thinking also changes, however, through the heart's influence. It learns from the heart to be more creative, generative, and sun-filled. To practice heart thinking one must be in the region of the threshold and in the "belt of lies" and assailed by illusion. Gradually head and heart together acquire an instinct for the truth.

Our age demands a new kind of thinking that is open to much more than materialism and reductionism is able to consider. Yet this kind of thinking needs objective standards of truth, just as thoughts of the material world must be objective. Objective heart thinking is the only thing that can win the kind of spiritual insights capable of grasping the question of what it is to be born a human being, which I said one needs to know to make an informed decision on the issue of abortion. In the process of reproduction, the seer can report seeing how a seed—a phenomenon of soul and spirit, not of the Earth—united itself with the bodily forces built up through evolution over millions of years. The process is hidden to physical eyes, but transparent to eyes of the spirit. Heart thinking—the thinking of the threshold—gradually makes such mysteries transparent. Chapter 4 will consider the process of what needs to be done to begin acquiring such a faculty to make our thinking true.

In the works of great spiritual teachers, we can find help in opening our spiritual organs of perception. Such a handbook appeared at the beginning of the twentieth century: Rudolf Steiner's *How to Know Higher Worlds.*[5] This essential text provides exercises, given with complete transparency so that those practicing them know exactly what they are doing. We are not following this particular path in the *Roadmap*. The path of the *Roadmap* is parallel to that one. It starts not with exercises of perception, but with the transformation of thinking through qualities of heart and will and through one's encounters in the region of the threshold. The two paths overlap and are complementary—both are the products of a new consciousness that is increasingly present in people today as the right and natural next step of human evolution. Individuals must find the ways to answer the questions that arise in them, and the existential questions that surface for people in this age more and more involve learning how to take hold of totally new insight from across the spiritual threshold. A power is building from the collective weight of so much inquiry into phenomena and processes that the intellect alone cannot penetrate.

Today it's as if a renaissance is being prepared everywhere through the destruction of much that has passed its "use-by" date. The consequences of the way we have been living confront us everywhere: pollution, global warming, corporate crime, poverty and homelessness, nuclear proliferation, surveillance and privacy issues, media disinformation, and much more. Such issues reflect the kind of people we have become and demonstrate the absolute need for change. Many young people recognize this, but those who do something about it will be in the minority, though progress invariably begins with a few. This minority of young people who use their hearts for thinking are our hope for the future. They will be furiously opposed by the old dinosaur order, but evolution is on the side of the new.

We have chosen to be alive in the twenty-first century and need to encounter the forces of the old order. Learning to bring life into what has become dead is the way that we will grow, and a certain struggle for truth is necessary for all those who wish to practice the new way of thinking with their heart. The next chapter is written as a stimulus toward learning how to think beyond the threshold. That is indeed the purpose of this whole book. We do not need more books that spin theories taken from the facts of this world alone; what we need are ideas through which we can develop new spiritual faculties. And for that we need to know more about the threshold itself and what goes on in that mysterious place.

As at the end of chapter 1, you may find it fruitful to prepare for the next stage of your journey by reminding yourself that you are equal to any situation you will meet. When thought is forced to go over the threshold, many temptations arise. What role should a dream, for example, play in our inquiries? A dream is a kind of message—we do well not to ignore them when they seem significant, but we tread dangerous ground if we take all our dreams as literal truth. We may be asked, for example, to put our faith in mediums and the like. Although insights can come from such sources, dreams and mediums offer no more than a means of getting information from outside sources. Experts, whether they receive information consciously or unconsciously, can offer new views, but only our own discrimination can tell us what is true and what is false. Renew your faith in the powers, which need to grow stronger. Live your life rightly and be active and creative in your thinking, and those processes will indeed become stronger and more active. Everything that happens to you will be beneficial according to how you meet it in your soul. On the stormy seas of the unknown, the compass that directs you will be found only within yourself—*your* hands, *your* head, *your* heart.

SUMMARY OF CHAPTER 3: THE NATURE OF THE THRESHOLD

The human being moves in the activity of thinking between two realms that can be called nature and spirit. Abstract thoughts can teach us only about what is dead. To become active in the region of the threshold and to think in a way that corresponds to what is alive, thinking needs to be imbued with qualities of heart and will. In the relationship between thought and the brain—the brain as a kind of receptor of thoughts, not as the creator of thoughts.

Thoughts about spirit—we need to be able to solve the questions they pose for us and how this brings us up against a threshold whereby these questions cannot be immediately answered. The region of uncertainty, called by Rudolf Steiner the belt of lies, as a borderland area located between what can be answered by commonsense and the methods of inquiry of the senses and the place in which eternal reality is to be found. This borderland between two realms is a region of great tension. Positivism grounds us on quantifiable reality alone; reductionism treats everything as if it were a dead body. Reductionist thinking, employed outside of its valid area, is turning our world into a graveyard. "Dead, materialistic thinking fills the world with corpses because it treats the world as a corpse. It has no feeling for life." The Large Hadron Collider in Geneva, Switzerland, as an extreme example of reductionist, mechanistic thought.

Against this we need to cultivate the thinking of the heart, but between head and heart there is great possibility for error. People who wish to learn to think with the heart have to undergo a kind of apprenticeship in the region of the threshold. "Complete security of truth can be won only from taking one's questions across the threshold and bringing back the answers from the other side." How people today are being thrown by life into such trials in order to learn how to think with the heart. The dangers of abstraction and "super-materialism." Objective heart thinking when head and heart work together in the region of the threshold to acquire an instinct for truth. Two different paths to the spirit—one starting with perception and the senses, and the other with the development of thinking in the realm of the threshold. In this second path, individuals need to work out of their own faculties of truth.

4

Into the Labyrinth

"There is no doubt—the One World is forming. Probably this is the most revolutionary event in the history of the world."
—Erich Fromm[1]

"For our wrestling is not against flesh and blood, but against the principalities, against the powers, against the world's rulers of the darkness of this age, and against the spiritual forces of wickedness in high places."
—St. Paul[2]

"Which government is best? That which teaches us to govern ourselves."
—Goethe[3]

"If you board the wrong train, it's no use running down the aisle in the opposite direction."
—Dietrich Bonhoeffer[4]

It was said at the end of the previous chapter that we need the struggles of the world if we are to go correctly on our path. We cannot avoid work in the world, and the most fruitful kind of work will arise where the impulses to act come from across the threshold. A certain struggle for truth is needed by those who wish to practice thinking with the heart. This chapter is written as a stimulus to learning how to function within the region of the threshold and to suggest how activity across the threshold can become fruitful for our day-to-day activity.

There may be those who began this book believing that people on a spiritual path should be hermits and disinterested in worldly affairs; those people may have stopped reading by this point. This book is my personal view, not on spirituality in general but on walking the path in the twenty-first century. Regardless of what happened in the past, I believe it is impossible today to develop our potential correctly without bumping into some of the issues discussed in this chapter. The path is one of gradually increasing our awareness, concern, and ability to be effective for the wellbeing and future of the Earth. By now it should be clear that the very reason to walk a path of inner development consciously is not for your own benefit primarily but for that of the whole Earth. The path of today cannot be separated from what we do in our daily life. If we are to be effective in our life's work, it is necessary that we know something of the drama going on behind world events, that we have a feeling for what is trying to be born into the world and know how to support this in our own thoughts and actions.

This is one reason for looking at world events—to see how we can most effectively be in harmony with the events of the time and contribute to human progress. The second reason is that anyone who begins to cross the threshold—as all humanity is now doing, consciously or unconsciously—inevitably encounters thought forms from the belt of lies. These thought forms will arise before those who are on the path to freedom, almost as if sent by order of our higher self to test our sense for truth. Arising as a plague from the media and many other sources, we can expect to encounter them constantly as a test of our ability to walk the path. Swallow some of those lies, and we will deviate from our path. Encounters with falsehoods test all our faculties across the threshold. Can we be open to life and yet discriminate between what is true and what is untrue? Can we develop an instinct for the truth? How we deal with what comes to us in the region of the threshold will determine to a great extent the kind of progress we will be able to make on our life's path. The inner path is also an outer path. Will your life be a narrow series of events in which you meet people and have experiences significant to your personal destiny, but in which your thoughts and actions have little importance for the world? Or are you able to fit your life into the overall pattern of world evolution?

When someone takes up the business of walking a spiritual path there is one danger that is greater than all others. It is not that they may be tempted to do evil—it is that existence at the region of the threshold has the tendency to give anyone an inflated sense of themselves and their own particular concerns. Personality inflation in a spiritual sense is something far different from simple vanity or single-mindedness, and no sensible person can ever say they are immune to it. We need certain trials to be able to work our way through the landscape of temptation that confronts us beyond the threshold. Grappling for clarity about the Earth with thoughts carried over the threshold is a slow process in which one's powers of discrimination and judgment are checked by universal laws. The way you choose to live your life is a matter about which a myriad of powers in this world and beyond have considerable vested interest. Only if you are really open to the world beyond the threshold—and prepared for the shocks that you will encounter there—will your life be enlarged in such a way that you become a conscious participant in the destiny of our time. Only if, in that openness, you sharpen your sense for truth as you come up against many half-truths and lies will you avoid being swept off course so that your life loses its relevance to the destiny of the Earth. This is the drama behind the life story of every human being. "To be or not to be?" What will you be open to? What will you become?

The "shocks" that await those who venture across the threshold are considerable, and we should not underestimate the effect that things we will see may have upon us. The spiritual teacher Rudolf Steiner, whose words can be trusted to come directly from his experience, had this to say:

> The world's powers are both destructive and constructive; the fate of sense-perceptible beings is to arise and pass away. The initiate must see and understand how these forces and this fate work themselves out. For this, the veil that lies before our spiritual eyes in ordinary life must be removed. Of course, we ourselves are closely interwoven with these forces and with fate. Our individual natures, like the world, contain destructive and constructive forces. As initiates, our own souls will be revealed before our seeing eyes as nakedly as all other things.
>
> Students must not lose strength in the face of such self-knowledge. They must come to meet it with a surplus of forces. In order to have this surplus, we must learn to maintain our inward calm and certainty in difficult life situations and cultivate an unshakable trust in the good powers of existence.[5]

I began my first draft of this chapter eight years ago, giving a lot of information on world events, with considerable emphasis on the events of September 11, 2001. Rewriting it recently, I removed most of that, not because I changed my mind about what happened or have come to feel that 9/11 is no longer relevant. September 11, 2001, is fundamentally important to our world because, through that event, forces that usually remain hidden, though they are always working from the shadows to influence world events, became clearly visible. Murders of key people have long influenced what happens in the world. But with 9/11, all this is taken to another level. September 11, 2001, was audacious; the evidence for skullduggery, committed by the very same powers responsible for its investigation, is simply overwhelming. Skyscrapers have never collapsed directly downward ("into their own footprint" and at the speed of gravity with no resistance beneath them) because of fire on the floors above. On September 11, 2001, this happened not once, not twice, but three times—three buildings toppled directly downward after aircraft hit two of them. Some kind of controlled demolition by *someone* who had access to the buildings is the only logical explanation. At the time of publication, some two thousand architects and engineers have come forward to state that the official explanation of how the three buildings fell is physically impossible.[6] Anyone with common sense who reads the reports on their website with an open mind will be forced to share their skepticism. Yet today, 9/11 and the taint of "conspiracy theory" still casts a spell that many people cannot get past. Those who speak out risk losing their jobs—and sometimes their lives—while most people simply do not speak of it.

However, something as big as this cannot really be hidden, can it? It surely can't be hidden forever? Yet, what really happened remains hidden to the majority of people. Although freedom of thought is a human right for which thousands have given their lives, vast multitudes of human beings have imposed upon themselves a prohibition against considering the events around 9/11. The term *conspiracy theory* is the first discouragement to independent thought. Incredible as this is, serious consideration of 9/11 as an act of mass murder by an organized group from within the United States remains fundamentally off limits to mainstream dialogue.

I rewrote my chapter because it's not my purpose to prove this. Anyone who has doubts or questions can consult many good sources of information; people have taken considerable personal risk and made great sacrifice to ensure that the information is available. Without going into detail, let us just mention the theologian David Ray Griffin,[7] who soberly analyzed the administration's own investigation; Steven Jones,[8] a physicist from Bringham Young University, who looked into the mechanics of how steel-core buildings could be made to fall; or the late Mike Ruppert, whose book *Crossing the Rubicon*[9] ties it all together. I can leave it to people far more knowledgable than I am to shine light on what happened on September 11, 2001. My theme here is the relevance of this for those of us who take a spiritual path in a time when such events take place.

From events such as 9/11 and fabrications that surround them, we can see that the world is wrapped in great swathes of falsehood. It is even possible to consider the whole twenty-first-century consumer culture as one great tissue of lies. This fact has to be confronted soberly. Those who understand this aspect of the world must remain effective in it. The spiritual path always leads seekers to the point where they feel that solid ground has been taken away from them; they have to function without the usual supports. We can be thankful to be born in such a time as this; ordinary life, if we do not simply go with the flow but work to wake up to it, will produce such a crisis. Realizing the great power of evil in the world is a crisis and it's impossible to calculate how many people have committed suicide through coming to some degree of awareness of it, unprepared and with insufficient protection. But those who walk the path consciously cannot say they are unprepared for what they will see. Meeting evil is an important part of the path.

The falsehood of 9/11 is a consequence of the activity of the belt of lies (first mentioned in chapter 3). It affects us all, whether we are aware of it or not, but for those on the spiritual path it must be resolved. Whether or not you choose to debunk falsehood in the outer world (a difficult task because the liars have the power of the press and are sophisticated in their practices), those who have stepped onto the threshold are going to encounter this web of deceit and will not be able to get far unless they are able to sort out what is true and what is false for themselves.

That there is so much power living in the belt of lies is a necessity of our time. Just as the hammer needs the resistance of the anvil to feel its own power, so, too, the thinking and feeling of our true ego (our "I") need the resistance of the belt of lies to become what they have the capacity to become. Deceit damages billions, yet once we become aware of it we can be grateful to it rather than losing our strength in anger, grief, and despair at the injustice of it. The all-pervading falsehood of our civilization is actually the means by which we can find strength and courage to stand more strongly in the light of truth.

I pointed out in chapter 3 that one of the great phenomena of our time is the need in this century to overcome the materialistic, reductionist thinking that denies realities we know are significant. Because it denies our everyday experience and our commonsense, reductionist thinking is a kind of lie. Without seriously considering what they are doing, many people fall for it. Reductionist thinking is the source of all other lies, because it denies reality to the soul and spirit, and in our time soul and spirit are working to shape the world in an entirely new direction, and they need to be recognized for this to occur.

In thoughts about the inorganic world, the damage done by reductionism may not be particularly obvious, but when reductionism is applied to the *living* world—and especially to human affairs—then something with tremendous potential for destruction enters our world. Reductionist thinking is fine for the construction of an efficient traffic-flow system in downtown New York or for the development of the next stage of laser weaponry, but ideas that deny life, soul, and spirit play havoc when applied to the natural and human worlds in which life, soul, and spirit exist.

One way to understand the present political situation is to see how a new kind of holistic thinking that does not damage life, soul, and spirit is trying to enter every facet of the world and overcome the tyranny of reductionism. Feeling threatened by this, advocates of the old way of thinking will not make way willingly for the new, but fight with the energy of a cornered beast to keep every scrap of their power.

Everything is about power to those who try to hold on to it. A certain oilman of the twentieth century is reported to have said, "The meek shall inherit the Earth—but not its mineral rights."[10] When we enter the arena of powerful vested interests we may need to fight them literally—in a court of law, if not on the street. But more important than this is the need to understand how the future belongs to a different kind of power, one that appears powerless to representatives of the old power structures. We take away the power of the old when we come to recognize the pitiful limitations of its worldview. A present-day American president may be one of the most powerful men who has ever lived in respect to the number of people he can kill if he has a mind to, but the system he represents is still a pathetic, doomed empire that cannot survive because it is fantastically out of touch with the evolutionary direction of world events. Evolution demands continual change in how we think and act—sometimes in the form of a steady progression, sometimes as a sudden leap. The old system is as doomed as the dinosaurs were, but it has no intentions of going quietly, and only great acts of human courage and creativity will enable it to let go and pass on.

It is a fact that materialism—seeing the world exclusively in terms of material cause and effect and denying soul and spirit—is here to stay; we can expect that it will only grow stronger for hundreds of years. We who have seen that the emperor has no clothes and that the ideas of materialistic thought are a tissue of falsehoods with nothing propping them up or holding them together may still have to suffer through much greater devastation, and this will test our strength and our faith in spiritual sources of renewal. This is the age into which we were born. The *Roadmap* can't prescribe to anyone how to act in the situations they encounter through their own destiny and the destiny of the times. Reality is tough, but never lose sight of the world; care deeply about all that happens in the world but remember to lift your head above it. The sources of renewal available to us are inexhaustible. No matter what happens to us on our outer path, we can expect the power of spiritual renewal to enter our life in an ever-stronger fashion. Sometimes all we can do is plant seeds into the soil of devastation, but those seeds are important; we can be certain that they will sprout one day into actions that make a difference.

Representatives of the power structures of a previous century frame their actions as if they are initiating things in harmony with the spirit of the times, but what they actually bring about is a kind of caricature of what is trying to emerge. The ways such people have represented the idea of *globalization* is a good example. We live in a time when many barriers of the past are broken down—a time of great communication, in which it is both possible and necessary for world citizens to recognize a shared spirit of humanity running through all nations. If the needs of the time were served truly by governments striving to facilitate a natural evolutionary progression among all nations, then each country would be able to journey without interference on its own particular pathway. Countries travel a path just as individuals do. The progress of one country would give it special ability to serve other countries, just as humanity is served every time individuals step out on their own personal, developmental journey. All countries would grow strong and self-governing and be able to develop their own unique potential, and the world as a whole would be far better off than with a few nations prospering at the expense of others. This was the vision of Dag Hammarskjöld, the second leader of the United Nations, whose words about the path served as an introduction to this book. During his tenure as Secretary General of the United Nations, he was murdered to prevent him from putting his ideas into practice; but since his death his vision has penetrated through to many people.[11]

Dag Hammarskjöld's vision of the human community is the "One World" described by Erich Fromm at the opening of this chapter. It is not the vision shared by most of the major powers of this present sociopolitical and economic world order. Although there is nothing like total agreement on how things should be, many of the biggest players of the Western world are working together toward what they call a "New World Order" created in their image. Their world order is the polar opposite of the One World vision of Dag Hammarskjöld and Erich Fromm. What they have worked for can be examined in their statements about what they believe. In *The Grand Chessboard* by Zbigniew Brzezinski, we read firsthand from this influential thinker's philosophy of power and control—his advocacy for the maintenance of hegemony and "empire" at all costs. A single example from many possible is this description of basic principles:

> To put it in a terminology that harkens back to the more brutal age of ancient empires, the three grand imperatives of imperial geostrategy are to prevent collusion and maintain security dependence among the vassals, to keep tributaries pliant and protected, and to keep the barbarians from coming together."[12]

This is the voice of the "New World Order" leaders, and it is unashamedly against individual freedom and the good of the whole. The elite believe they are the only people who should be allowed to follow their own free will, and that everyone else must be forcibly kept in their place.

The spirit of the present time leads us into greater communication and connection among nations and races. Reactionary leaders also work within the framework of the realities of the times but divert it into different directions. Their concept of "globalization" becomes distorted. This is how the old power structures work. There is evolution and there is counter-evolution. Much that is filled with the goodness of the future is corrupted by what the leaders of the old power structures do to it. Through their activity, everything is distorted as it passes through the belt of lies. Call it a conspiracy theory if you want; it is also simply the perfectly understandable will of the old, functioning at every level, to hang on to power at all cost.

Before Erich Fromm's *One World* can manifest, many representatives of power in today's world must relinquish power or at least use it in a very different way, as servants rather than as rulers. If power is forcefully taken from them by individuals who merely transfer power to themselves, nothing changes. *One World* is based on something other than power. Dag Hammarskjöld expressed it in a 1958 speech in Cambridge: "The principle of power has to give way to the principle of justice."[13] People who do not understand the way our world is woven together with a spiritual reality dismiss this as utopian thinking. Who relinquishes world power voluntarily? Nonetheless, those who understand the interconnectedness of matter and spirit know that this is the only way human beings can live fulfilling lives in full human dignity.

The majority of those who wield power today are going against the evolutionary progression of our age. They are doomed, just as the communists were in 1989 with the fall of the Berlin Wall. If they are to continue in the driver's seat, they will have to create more events such as 9/11. Fear must be manufactured, sources of fuel controlled, civil liberties eliminated, and destabilizing world chaos generated. Because these people must be seen as doing good, everything they say and do is always accompanied by a litany of lies that lull, spawn hatred, and create fear. Behind it all is desperation, longing, and regret. "The old order changeth, yielding place to new."[14] This is the long-term picture of our time, but an easy and quick victory over the old guard cannot be expected; we should not expect to witness some voluntary surrender of power. On every level there rages a most savage battle costing millions of lives. The tyrant, the other emperor with no clothes, is desperate, insane, and terribly unhappy.

The world of the old nineteenth-century capitalist order has become a monster that consumes itself in order to survive. It marches toward economic collapse through creating major world imbalance, and the chaos of such a breakdown—fear and greed contending with each other—will be a smokescreen for other acts of criminality that it will perpetrate. What shall we do about this? Shall we try and oppose it? Is it possible to conceive of a new form of world governance that is in harmony with the true spirit of the times? Or do we have a different task?

For a start, there are no "shoulds" in a path of free will. We will do what the voice of love within us suggests in any given situation. But we must also recognize what is going on, and studying what is happening in the world can make us feel angry and powerless. Let us admit that we cannot change the world. We can diagnose that there is something (the kind of thinking employed by the old order) at the root of world stagnation, and we can be agents for change. However, what we do will be small and probably go unnoticed. Part of the drama of this fourth chapter is that we must endure the trial of coming face-to-face with our own limitations.

Through confronting our limitations we find our humanity. Looking truthfully at the world situation, we see—on one level—that we cannot actually make a difference. These things are just too big for us as individuals. Yet the admission of powerlessness is an important stage on the path. Something can work *through* us if we give it opportunity. The dignity of human beings has to do with how we are able to become instruments through which something greater than ourselves can work in the world.

If we are honest and if we carry the insight of chapter 2 into this situation—that we are not separate from anything around us—then we know that we cannot simply sit on the sidelines and claim that we are not involved. The problems of the Earth are of our own making. By the clues of our own life events we can even come to a feeling for how our mistakes in previous lives have contributed to the overall problem. We need to do what we can to set things right. *But what can we do?*

The first thing we can do is to counter falsehood. The events of 9/11 are very obvious examples of the activities of evil—visible yet hidden from mainstream world understanding. On your spiritual path you will have to work just as hard to discriminate when dealing with countless other issues, large and small. Since 9/11 it has become quite clear: every individual, if they are going to become free agents, working effectively in what they undertake, must grapple with truth and falsehood in the affairs of the world. Even if nothing happens visibly, doing this is still a deed on the world stage because thought is a reality. One person coming to clarity about something may turn out to be more powerful than a thousand who are simply going along with what they have been told to think.

World events are metaphors for the transformation individuals undergo. The change from nineteenth to twenty-first century shows us outwardly the movement from imperialism to something entirely new. Imperialism and colonialism in their day were simply the way things happened. Bad as they were, we do not have to judge them by the standards of today. World events worked through them, and in some ways they were in harmony with the spirit of their times. But to continue with imperialism or the kind of thinking that lies behind imperialism in *our* day is a most terrible injustice. Imperialism is still very much present in the twenty-first century, acting as a kind of invisible, malevolent puppet-master. It is there behind our entrenched power structures. Much of the continent of Africa is being dominated just as much today as two centuries ago, and there is something very evil in this. If it takes such injustice to make our civilization work, then doesn't this show that contemporary civilization in its present form is not viable. We must learn to recognize injustice in all its disguises and oppose it. Very often we will not be able to do this directly in the outer world—but there is always a place where we can immediately set to work to create a better world. That place is within us.

One's own soul—yes, we are back to that, for it is the place where world event and spiritual process overlap. The drama of the present evolutionary moment is all about the need for us to counter decadent forces from the past first of all within ourselves—to descend into the darkness of our own will and bring healing there. We are all today like Prospero who, at the end of *The Tempest*, admits of Caliban that, "This thing of darkness I acknowledge mine."[15] When we become whole we can help to create health and wholeness in the Earth. The redemption of the Earth—like the redemption of Caliban as one of its fallen creatures—will not happen overnight. First we have to feel the enormity of what we are attempting to change. We have to know that we, too, have a Caliban within us. The more accurately we can live into the hopelessness of this situation, the more that new sources of healing will be able to arise in us in the fullness of time.

Is this not a clue as to why so many people cannot confront the evil of 9/11 objectively? Subconsciously they know that to understand it all fully and to be able to make a creative response to it they would have to make a journey into the evil within themselves. This can certainly be done, but it needs courage, and many will avoid doing it if they can. Going within is an endurance of negative capability within the belt of lies. It is a painful and lonely thing to do, but it is through doing this that a person becomes able to stand alone as a free individuality. To work to become free is a necessary part of our evolution—one very important aspect of the reason we find ourselves here on the Earth today. The myths, fairytales, and great stories of the past have been a preparation for us to connect with our destined tasks—those that arise before us with a kind of historical inevitability about them. Is it not a wonderful thing to grapple with the self-chosen ordeals of one's own destiny. People are inspired to do this because they are longing to become someone through whom the rising wave of a new world evolution is able to flow. They do it not because anyone tells them they must but because it is something they long to do in order to be true to themselves.

Where are we? This chapter describes a process that is a very important part of the present-day path. Our discrimination must be tested, and this happens in the region of the belt of lies. The previous chapter discussed the fact that we have difficulty taking thoughts across the threshold, because our power to hold on to them in that region is not yet strong enough. Standing as naked individuals and living with questions that require inner research enables us to find that strength. The heart must be directed in the right way or one's thoughts will veer madly in weird directions. There will never be divine intervention in the world that saves believers and banishes infidels into eternal perdition. Human intervention is needed. The gods stand back, ready to help but wanting us to work out of our own freedom. We need to see the matter truly to be able to lend our assistance to the work of others. "One person alone can do nothing—only those who unite themselves with others at the right place and time."[16]

The great conspiracy is not political but personal; it stops individuals from understanding the drama of their own life and from crossing the threshold. What one person can do against the criminals who set up 9/11 is limited. They have been given opportunity for a time to wage their work of destruction, and only slowly will others wake up to what is going on. But the conspirators can be unmasked in one's inner self. They are the powers that try to prevent your rightful crossing of the threshold, and they are doing their work at this very moment within you by conjuring fear, confusion, doubt, guilt, despair, egoistic desire, or some other "human, all-too-human" emotion that can block you from attaining what is rightfully yours.

We cannot avoid work in the world. We are called upon to help the peoples of this Earth transition out of the age of materialistic darkness into a new activity of collegiality with the spiritual world. As Dag Hammarskjöld said, "In our era, the road to holiness necessarily passes through the world of action."[17] It is no more an idle dream to imagine what the Earth can become than it is to hold a seed in your fingers and imagine a lily or a pine tree hidden within it. This world contains its next level, but our activity is needed for it to attain that new level. Our own spiritual work cannot be fruitful unless it makes us better at serving other people and at performing the tasks we choose to act in partnership with them. But because we are attempting to achieve goals that are much broader than the goals people generally are trying to achieve, we need not be too fixed on the result. In the world there will be setbacks, but the aims we carry will go on. Sometimes the opposition to what we would like to do is simply too strong. Increasingly, we see that it is these times in particular that can strengthen our will. When it comes to doing things that are of service to progressive evolution in the world, our success will often depend upon factors we simply can't influence. In this world the biological and intellectual human being fights against the spiritual and moral one. So many of the great leaders of the twentieth century were assassinated—Gandhi, Hammarskjöld, John and Robert Kennedy, Dr. Martin Luther King Jr., Malcolm X, John Lennon. They were individuals who had achieved much and who carried further potential. That they could not go further in the public arena is a picture of how powerful the opposition to their work is in our time. But such deaths allow the martyr's power to spread out into the whole. We have all assumed a little of the responsibility for humanity that such people carry.

In the twenty-first century, a critical mass is building in the spiritual life of humanity. This power will bring about the necessary turn toward new ways of life. If we are engaged in a certain task in the world—one based on thought that is not reductionist but is of the heart—we may not be able to accomplish our aim to our full satisfaction. The world is caught in the grip of materialism and this is not going to change overnight. It will change in the longer term—of that we can be certain—but we may not yet be up to the task, our resolve may lack the necessary strength, or the timing may simply be unfavorable. In this situation, merely to carry the big picture of what can be done will bring achievement of one kind or another, and this book is all about showing how we can be effective.

In her prison cell in Rouen in 1431, Joan of Arc, nineteen years of age and facing the power of a system devised to crush individuality and turn innocence into guilt, was assured by spiritual "voices" that, if she persevered in her resistance, she would win a great victory. The voices were correct, but it was not the victory that Joan, hoping for release from her imprisonment, could understand at first. We might find ourselves in similar situations—needing to endure without the consolation of hearing the encouragement of others, but simply through the force of our own intuition telling us we are doing the right thing. In the outer world, small things matter very much when done in the right spirit. The way Joan refused to back down from the truth while outwardly enduring powerlessness can inspire us to act on our own will to do good in the face of resistance.

On the level of our own souls, we can indeed win the great victory and we can win it now. We cannot blame inadequate resources or colleagues; our estate is the battleground of our own soul; we own it and carry full responsibility for what takes place there. Everything that happens in our inner life can be a step forward on the path. In contrast to the physical world, in our soul we can unmask the conspiracy against evolutionary currents from the spiritual world. If we want to change the world, we must change ourselves. If we want to change ourselves, we must become active catalysts for evolutionary change in the world.

This chapter is the central one in a series of seven. Four, the number of the square, is the number of Earth—our ideals needing to be incarnated, our thoughts needing to go through the strengthening process that encountering resistance provides. "We are not earthly beings having a spiritual experience but spiritual beings having an earthly experience."[18] One day the Earth will be superseded, and nothing visible will remain. In some ways what we see today is most definitely *maya*, or illusion. Yet our spiritual path must take us right down into the earth. We will become aware of what is real only if we grapple with the illusions. If the present condition of the Earth is avoided, if we do not base our work on what we face now and the needs of the present situation, then our path becomes false and will not help human evolution but create further difficulties.

This is what I felt needed to be said about the tension between Heaven and Earth and where we stand in the midst of it. We shall take a step into the unknown in the next chapter.

Summary of Chapter 4: Into the Labyrinth

The encounter with falsehood as a test of one's faculties across the threshold. The danger of personality inflation across the threshold. Standing up to the necessary temptations that arise at the threshold. September 11, 2001, a time when evil emerged into the open. How the whole of our culture can be seen to be enmeshed in great falsehood. People who confront this falsehood need to do so carefully to avoid losing effectiveness in the world. Meeting evil is a necessary part of the path today. Meeting power with powerlessness. Remembering inexhaustible sources of spiritual renewal. True globalization and its double—the false "New World Order" as described by Zbigniew Brzezinski.

Discovering how to counter the false approach to globalization by confronting our own limitations and connecting with our deepest humanity. Creating a better world through what we do in our own souls, where world events and spiritual processes overlap. Being able to say, as Prospero said of Caliban, "This thing of darkness I acknowledge mine." The courage needed to become a free individuality. Joan of Arc as an example to us today of how to stand up for truth when facing forces that are more powerful in worldly terms than we are. And how upon the inner plane we can indeed win a victory and unmask the enemies of right evolutionary growth. "If you want to change the world, change yourself. If you want to change yourself, become an active catalyst for evolutionary change in the world." How this fourth chapter is all to do with being true to the Earth.

5

Cross Now!

"*The old is dying, the future not yet born. Who will fetch the man with the lamp?*"

—M. Burton, *The Green Snake*[1]

"*Quietly and unceasingly [to] direct the greatest force upon the smallest point...*"

—Goethe[2]

"*Yoga is the suppression of the oscillations of the mental substance.*"

—Patanjali[3]

"*What we must learn in this age: to live out of pure trust without any security in existence—trust in the ever-present help of the spiritual world.*"

—Rudolf Steiner[4]

This is meant to be more than just a book. I called it a "roadmap," and that may have raised expectations—a roadmap being something simple, practical, and easy to understand for most people. The realm that an individual travels while on a spiritual path is, however, not at all simple and will be found to take a lot longer than driving a few miles across town. I do not suggest that it is a simple journey, but perhaps this book can assist with an orientation by describing the terrain ahead. This is the purpose of the first four chapters.

There are seven chapters in this roadmap. Seven is a number that crops up frequently in science and nature. Among many other things, seven is the number of steps needed for any spiritual transformation. Early alchemists outlined the path required for human beings to make a conscious relationship to the spiritual world (or for two people to make a relationship with each other). Nowadays, most people know very little about alchemy but, if you were to ask people about it, I think most would say that it was a rather dubious precursor of chemistry that had something to do with making gold from a base material. The idea of making gold has remained in people's awareness, whereas the true purpose of the alchemical transformation process has been largely forgotten. When alchemy was at the cutting edge of enlightenment, the idea of literally manufacturing gold was actually a red herring—a distraction that weeded out lesser alchemists and concealed from most people the main business of the work.

What is the real task of alchemy? In its true form alchemy was never about making gold, but is a path of bringing about an interaction, or "marriage," between the human soul and the spiritual world. At the start of our journey on the alchemical path, we think only in human terms, while the spiritual seems far removed. Gradually, as the path is traveled and the various stages of it are experienced, the two grow closer and certain changes happen to both. Human earthliness begins to change when faced by a world ruled by entirely different laws from those of Earth. We change; if the path is good, we maintain our connection to the Earth but begin to live in both worlds, Heaven and Earth. In the final, seventh step, the marriage takes place; the spiritual world unites with the human soul. The two coexist, no longer separated or in conflict or in a relationship whereby one destroys or dominates the other, but in newly created harmony.

Similarly, the journey mapped out in this book is also alchemical in nature. Each chapter has a theme that sets the conditions for taking another step on the path. For most of us, the path is not linear and sequential. It may twist and turn and seem to double back on itself; things seem to happen out of order. Nevertheless, seven archetypal processes of the alchemical path do lie behind the seeming chaos of our wandering steps. In the first four chapters we began to become familiar with them.

Chapter 4 discusses the "death" stage, *mortificatio*, also called *nigredo*, or blackening. It is the step that seems not to move us forward at all. When we are at the point of *nigredo*, we feel stuck and realize we have to backtrack and make a new start. We cannot avoid the fourth step; we need it to gain the strength for the fifth, which begins only when we have spent enough time in the realm of blackness. In this view of the path, the realm of blackness is the belt of lies, and what we bring back from it is the heightened sense of judgment needed to cross the threshold.

Through chapter 4, I hope it has become clear for you the process by which a soul gains strength through learning to discriminate across the threshold. Of course, there are other ways the soul grows strong. Discriminating among political ideas—some true, some not—is only one way. However, this is a path that allows us to remain faithful to the Earth, and human initiations today are quite different from what they were in the past. In earlier times, people could work on inner development in a monastery, cave, or temple in blissful ignorance of the world outside. Today, being on the path means working to transform not just yourself but also the Earth. Much darkness has been brought to the Earth—physically, psychically, and spiritually—and no one who sets out on a spiritual quest can ignore the need to do everything possible to set it right.

The belt of lies presses in on us at every moment of our lives. Most people sleep through this, but those who awake must work hard to clear the air around them. It is necessary to attain a degree of insight into what works for the good and what merely passes itself off as good while actually working against the time. "In our time," said Dag Hammarskjöld, "the way to holiness necessarily passes through the path of action."⁵ This is well worth repeating here. This is the spiritual path—actively working for and promoting the progressive powers of evolution. To know how to get to the root of all the abuse that has been inflicted upon the Earth means making your own soul into a crucible in which "good and evil" or "truth and untruth" encounter one another and attain a higher synthesis. A higher synthesis is not a simple defeat of evil by good. In the world this may need to happen but in the realm of the soul things are subtler.

Chapters 3 to 5 are concerned particularly with the phenomenon we call the threshold: in chapter 3, I introduced the threshold; in chapter 4, I have tried to show how the soul grows stronger through certain experiences across the threshold; in chapter 5, my goal is to demonstrate how the soul actually crosses.

Crossing the gulf is a great task. Can we do it in a single chapter? It will become clearer as we see the true nature of the crossing. There will be no flash of white light or voice of angels singing. We spend time in the region of the belt of lies and become stronger there. We encounter both true and false thoughts and simply pay attention to each and give them refuge in our soul. Nothing happens quickly; we have learned to practice negative capability and lost our impatience for quick answers. We know by having achieved this that it is something we will be doing for the rest of our life. By practicing in this way, we change. We learn to think with active discrimination instead of jumping to conclusions and holding incomplete ideas in our soul. Through a creative synthesis of what we have brought together in the soul, our thoughts will be entirely new. Something from across the threshold will have acted upon them and they will carry creative, healing power in them because of where they originated. We become human beings who do not need the prompts from others or Earth's support to act. We learn to live on the other side of the threshold and not be torn apart by the experience.

This is all possible today. Prior to the nineteenth century, spiritual thoughts were available to people who at first tended to take hold of them instinctively. Darwin and others questioned everything that was built around a naive trust in humanity's special place in the world. In essence, the scientists of the nineteenth century removed the spiritual from every place it can be found on the Earth except one. That one place is within the individual human being. Those today who have outgrown the security of their childhood confront a spiritually empty world. There is only one place where the spiritual can be found: within us. To learn how to think truly is to take hold of the spirit within. We must all do this from our own inner forces; it cannot be given by a guru or passed on through education, although good teachers can do much to prepare the way. It is not a possession but an *activity*, and we are the ones who must be active. What is it that one does to practice the right kind of activity?

In some form or another, those of us who wish to learn to create from the spirit within must practice meditation. In meditation we close ourselves off for a while from impressions of the surrounding world and enter our inner world consciously. The normal first encounter with the inner world involves all the involuntary mental processes in which our conscious inner activity plays no role. It may seem for a while as if we are moving backward, but let's examine what happens when we begin to meditate. The soul space we inhabit in meditation is where the great threshold crossing takes place.

This is not a meditation guide—whole books are devoted to that, and people spend lifetimes practicing. Rather, what follows is a simple description of some early experiences that people notice when meditating. I describe a simple form of meditation, with no prayers, visualizations, or mantras at the outset. It involves simply closing our eyes and going consciously into our inner world and observing what is happening there.

To begin with, all sorts of things arise from the unconscious: memories, associations, sense impressions, feelings, stray mental images, awareness of physiological processes, and so on. If you switch off the habitual response of judging them, you can observe them in a state close to the state of a dream. At first, when this state is entered, the natural tendency will be to get bored or fall asleep. Strengthening the soul, in such ways as was described in the previous chapter, will help you stay awake. And when you do this, you can observe what is occurring. You observe but you play no part in what is going on. No activity is arising out of your own volition. But there will probably be quite a lot taking place. You are not active except as an observer, but much is happening within you.

When you dream, you have no chance of taking any active part in the play of images that arise. Animals, in their everyday consciousness, have an inner life similar to ours when we dream. Images "happen" to them and they react. There is no conscious "I" within them that observes the pictures and then stands back to think about them. Since the nineteenth century, many psychologists and scientists have tried to persuade us that there is no difference between our thinking and what goes on in the consciousness of an animal. In trance and daydream, yes, our consciousness is similar to that of an animal. The first observation you can make in meditation is to watch that passive proliferation of mental images happening within you and know that this is close to the dream state of the animal. But from within, you can also observe the observer—that inner presence which the animal does not have.

No amount of persuasion will change the minds of those who have concluded that there is little difference between human and animal consciousness. However, we are not trying here to persuade anyone, but merely suggesting the practice of self-observation. In doing this, it is a matter for oneself alone. We will not convince anyone else, but we may convince ourselves. Not right away, however, because this is not an easy observation, but those who quietly practice what has been described will become able to make this observation for themselves. Moreover, because we are within the experience in meditation, we can gain greater certainty about what takes place within ourselves than we would have as a result of any perceptions of the outer world.

Self-consciousness is not just being aware of the mental oscillations within oneself without the will playing a part in their creation. Self-consciousness is being aware of a *self*—the "I," which has been busy observing, the self that stands separate to the processes occurring without its participation. When the "I" gets busy and acts, it directs activity toward something outside the self; it starts to *think*. Thinking is not easy to observe, because when you think it takes up all your consciousness. It is impossible to observe your thinking while thinking. However, we can practice it for a while and then step back and know that we have been active in creating thoughts. They haven't arisen passively within you as dream thoughts do (what nineteenth-century scientists might call thoughts "excreted from the brain"); rather, we are active in creating them.

The animal is never truly active—at least, no more than a dreamer or a person who is drunk. Consider a mouse, for example. Obviously, there is a tremendous amount of movement in its inner experience, but it is all *reaction*. When people are drunk or dreaming, they react to the things going on inside or outside of them. Those who are "awake" may still spend most of their time merely reacting, and in extreme cases may act just like an animal does.

However, from personal experience and from studying one's inner life, we can begin to perceive the difference between those times when we are merely reacting and when we are inwardly active.

It is extremely important to be clear about this; we experience inwardly that, yes, we have the dreaming consciousness of animals, but we can also awaken and become spiritually active. This is not something that can be proved; scientists who subscribe to the creed of reductionism cannot stand the thought that there is a part of us that is not subject entirely to material forces, and they will have various ways to explain the "illusion" of inner freedom. Their ideas may be very sophisticated, and we might even feel we couldn't begin to refute them on their own territory without a PhD or two in our arsenal. Nonetheless, in meditation and self-observation, this inner activity of the self can simply be experienced. Meditation is something we do to wake up. As we get better at it, we can awake more completely. Our consciousness can become so strong that we learn to be inwardly silent amid all our ongoing physiological processes and yet not fall asleep. The "oscillations of the mental substance" are stilled, yet the self remains awake. When this self takes hold of thoughts that have their origin in another world—one that is always present but rarely seen, just as the stars are present during the day but are not seen because of the sunny sky—the self has begun to complete its crossing and to arrive in the spiritual world.

In life, the soul always needs to be strengthened to maintain and increase awareness and greater wakefulness. Meditants do not remain merely observing themselves but begin to live in significant images or words, shifting the focus away from the self toward something that can connect to spiritual realities. Through the ages, inspired words have always been given to us by the great teachers of humanity. Some people will be stronger in the realm of inner pictures, others in sounds. Each will find their way, step by step, on the greatest adventure that life offers. One of the few rules is that the time for doing these practices should be limited so that they never become an escape from one's daily life and responsibilities. Meditation must enhance daily life and make us better at whatever we are called by life to do.

Our steps on the path must be continually renewed so that a pathway is gradually worn into the rock by the repeated recapitulation of our footsteps. At different levels and at different times in a person's biography, new steps will be called for, and taking those steps will require great effort. Moreover, we encounter many hindrances within ourselves: the animalistic world of reactions and urges, the dark lethargy of what circulates through us and overtakes us when we are out of tune with our higher self, and the jagged coldness and harshness of our soul when it judges others and stops caring for them. The tendency to fall asleep and to become reactive rather than creative is always present, but with perseverance it can become second nature to face life with a dynamism that helps us to step continually across that threshold.

The threshold is not crossed once and that's the end of it; rather, it moves and we must move with it. Doing so is a very energetic activity, but not in the ways required by mountaineering or a triathlon. One who has made treading the path and crossing the threshold second nature has an inner dynamism that is linked to a great capacity for maintaining inner peace. Dynamic activity and peacefulness combined may sound contradictory, but the threshold *is* a paradoxical place. Once we have learned how to cross it, peace will emanate from us into the world as an inner intensity of energy works within our soul. The two may also be reversed, with great energy working out into the world. That energy is not that of an enraged bull but of a conscious human being who acts from a well of peace that is at the very foundation of that person's being.

There is a certain *atmosphere of the threshold* that comes when one is not being rebuffed by it and hurled back, bleeding and raw, into the world. At first anyone who tries consciously to cross the thresholds of life will suffer many rebuttals, but with practice this can be transformed. Peace surrounds those who are able to cross. Life becomes richer and truer as the atmosphere of the threshold permeates our life and is allowed to radiate into the world. On the threshold, life certainly becomes harder, but also far richer and more meaningful.

> Life grows more radiant about me.
> Life grows more arduous for me—
> Grows more abundant within me.[7]

People today are being led quite naturally and inevitably toward the threshold. It still feels for us to be a strange and even terrifying place. In the past, we were carried by various supports, just as a child is watched over by its mother. Now we are alone, and the deepening solitude can be most painful to bear. When people have no sense of what is happening and what it is leading toward, they can be driven to despair and suicide. We should not underestimate what a terrible pain the experiences of the threshold can be. This *Roadmap* is written to offer knowledge of the path so that people who find themselves facing such pain in their souls can get a feeling for what is happening and how they can play a part in their own initiation. Much pain can be borne when a person sees the greater good that will arise from their sufferings. Those who know the trials of the threshold can relieve the pain of others, even when the suffering one is not prepared to hear anything of the threshold itself. Experiences from across the threshold, lived through rightly, give us the capacity to support other human beings. If we have learned how to live on the other side of the threshold, compassion for the struggles of others will be present in us in a way that others can feel. Whether those who suffer are aware of it or not, they will be affected by the support of one who understands how the pain of loneliness that they are experiencing can lead to something much greater in their life.

Humanity at this moment of evolution is outgrowing the need for the supports that carried it in the past. Though the process is painful and full of heartache and regret for what is being lost, we are learning gradually to feel at home in the atmosphere of the threshold and in the realm across the threshold. There is no security in going back to earlier forms of consciousness. The way forward is into the abyss and beyond this abyss. It is for human beings an entirely new consciousness. Stressful! Exciting! Terrible! Amazing! Inevitable! Do it now from your own free will or remain in your one-sidedness and have it done to you later in ways you will not be able to control.

There is a scene in the Gospels that can inspire us concerning the crossing that we make. This is the picture of Christ walking on the water.[5] In the story there is a storm. The disciples, who are on a boat, see Christ walking on the water, and one of them, Simon Peter, leaves the boat and attempts to walk on the surface of the waves toward him. At first he does so successfully, but the sight of the dark water beneath him causes him to panic and he starts to sink. Christ calms the waves and supports Peter, and they are soon back in the boat. It is a powerful picture of the inner world.

The area of the threshold we described as a bridge can resemble a stormy sea. Imagine being down in the black water. You are between two realms, neither on solid earth nor yet on the spiritual shore. Fear of drowning is a deep, primeval human response to such insecurity and risk. Being afraid will do us no good—we know that. But the ground below is giving way, and there is nothing there. Where do we find the support? We must learn that there is indeed support for us, but we will not find it beneath us. It is above; it is something that can meet us from the spiritual world. It will descend toward us if we lift our awareness to meet it. This is the new kind of ground to those who dare to cross the threshold—solid ground that will support us not from below but from above. With great courage we must reach up and take hold of it.

Whatever your personal beliefs, deep peacefulness can be felt from imagining the story of Christ walking on the water as intensely as you can—the boat, the disciples, the dark waves, the sensation of sinking, the fear of drowning. If these have been imagined as vividly as possible, we may feel the presence of the King of the Elements, who has complete command over wind and waves and supports us from above. This is an image that can work powerfully into our lives and give us courage when we need it. When we look at life with greater intensity and with the sensitivity of an *artist*, we will be able to find more pictures that give us what we need. As the ground inevitably gives way beneath us, we will not long for the lost road back but will find what supports us from the other shore, what calls us forward from the future, what calms the tempest in our soul and pours strength into our steps forward.

Living without support and moving toward and over the threshold is gradually now becoming second nature to an increasing number of pioneering individuals. Being at the vanguard of what is possible to humanity, such people need great courage and a strong grasp of reality and commitment to life as they step into the unknown. What they achieve will slowly become the possession of most people. No doubt there will be many crises surrounding the emergence of the new consciousness; we see it everywhere, and we can expect the chaos of unconscious threshold experiences in the world to become increasingly visible. However, as the ability to live "without security in existence" and to cross the threshold is attained by more and more of us, it will mark a new and joyful stage in human evolution.

Summary of Chapter Five: Cross now!

The structure of seven chapters as stages in an alchemical process. The fourth step was the "death step," *mortificatio* or *nigredo,* the step of blackening, and in this journey it is a picture of us becoming strong in our souls through confrontation with falsehood in the region of the belt of lies. The task of chapter 5 is to make the crossing over the threshold. Learning from the experience of the threshold to act without the prompting of the outer world and to stand on the other side of the threshold without being torn to pieces by the experience. During the nineteenth century, Darwin and others destroyed the old spirituality and since then there is only one place in which spirituality can genuinely be found: in ourselves. We must take hold of this spirituality by learning to think from our own inner forces.

A description of the first experiences of meditation. Observation of consciousness—the dream consciousness that is similar to that of animals, in which images arise in us and we are passive compared to self-consciousness in which we become aware of the self that is active in the way that the animal cannot be. Deepening meditation would involve stilling all inner activity and not falling asleep but, being strengthened to stay awake, arriving at last in a wholly spiritual reality. Crossing the threshold as a dynamic activity that has to be continually repeated. Human beings are slowly learning to feel at home in the region of the threshold.

The story of Christ walking on the water as a picture of us learning to live without firm support beneath us, the ability to find new, solid ground, not beneath but above us. Learning to live without security in existence.

6

The Heart Knows

"*Deep, deep within ourselves are buried tremendous creative powers and abilities. They are so powerful, so beautiful, that we are ashamed of them. This is the disease of our present age. And these creative powers will remain unused forever unless we open the doors into our treasure-house and search for them.*"

—MICHAEL CHEKHOV[1]

"*The force that through the green fuse drives the flower drives my green age.*"

—DYLAN THOMAS[2]

"*Be wise as serpents and innocent as doves.*"

—CHRIST, Gospel of St. Matthew[3]

This is a good place to consider the wholeness of our journey. The sixth step is closely related to the heart and the *thinking of the heart*. As we concentrated on the business of approaching and crossing the threshold in chapters 3, 4 and 5, we entered some arid and tortuous regions. Now it can seem to us that we are coming out of them, bearing within us all the strength and insight attained on the journey.

In the region of the heart the particular stages of the path can be appreciated and *felt* in their different qualities, one from the other. Things seem to happen chaotically in life ("shit happens") and often there seems to be no reason for life's vicissitudes, yet we can sometimes understand—especially a while later—that it really was not as random as we first thought.

To say that the alchemical path always has seven steps is strictly speaking not true. One only has to study old alchemical material to see that there was no such agreement among past alchemists and present-day scholars, and that many more than seven processes and stages are described. Nevertheless, this series of seven is in accordance with inner tradition and spiritual reality and is employed in this roadmap, because it can become a helpful tool for understanding our own life. It was presented imaginatively in Goethe's fairytale, *The Green Snake and the Beautiful Lily.* A longer description of the seven stages of the process can be found in Paul Marshall Allen's commentary on that fairytale.[4] It is also presented with great clarity in a work already mentioned, *The Chymical Wedding,* Christian Rozenkreutz's seven-day journey of initiation.

The path of life could be viewed in many other ways, but considering stages of the path in this particular sevenfold way helps us detect the inner form and meaning of our life. Nonetheless, life does not end at seven; it is a spiral and will reverse, jump stages, and repeat at new levels, but awareness of the stages in a form such as this can help us understand life's events and be more proactive in life.

The first stage is the situation of disorganization when all the different aspects of the human being are undifferentiated and in chaos. All new beginnings start at this point. Taking up a path is to begin to address that chaos. Chapter 1 describes the contemporary human being. If you read that chapter and remain open to some of its radical claims, you can begin this journey with me toward understanding your own path. You walk it every day with or without a roadmap, but this is intended to help you in turning your personal path into a more conscious initiation journey with greater understanding of the processes taking place behind the events of your life.

The second stage of the alchemical path can be summed up in the Latin word *sevaratio* (separation). By addressing chaotic elements, they begin to be differentiated. At this stage we have to make choices and exercise freedom rather than simply falling into the natural responses of addiction and naive fundamentalism that, to some extent, will take over the lives of those who choose simply to go along with the hormonal push-and-pull of stimulus and response. Freedom means saying no, being able to endure separation even though it can be painful.

A fusion of these separate elements takes place during the third stage of the path, *coniunctio*. Something new emerges from the tension of opposing elements. In this book that new something was described imaginatively as the ability to carry thoughts across the threshold.

The trials of this crossing are addressed in the fourth stage, which has been described and given the name *nigredo*, or blackening—meeting the forces of death.

Various names are given to the fifth stage, but what is important about it is to feel that, after the hard, jagged, and confrontational elements of the fourth stage, this is a softer, more "watery" experience. In life we sometimes fight battles until we are forced to let go. We can learn the art of when to fight and when to let go. Letting go does not have to be negative or defeatist; it can be part of the strategy of moving toward a goal but changing tactics, a kind of "tactical retreat."

On this fifth stage of the path, I realize that I am not alone. My wings are washed in healing waters and my aching heart is soothed and persuaded to have trust. The term *solutio* expresses how at this stage of the path I perceive that much that I had carried as conflict within myself is being dissolved by a force greater than myself. A catharsis is at work, healing on a level beyond ordinary consciousness. I feel something blessed happening to me and that I am changing. Images of water, of whiteness and being washed frequently appear at this stage of the path. On the spiritual path, individuals don't leap across the threshold out of their own energy or ability. We must learn that we do not possess the strength to do it alone. But the great crossing is nevertheless made; the darkest hour has passed and I feel blessed by a special grace that has come into my life and bestowed new energy upon me.

The sixth step is even more mysterious, and even less do we feel it taking place as something achieved by our own effort. The name *coagulatio* is given to a kind of condensation of what is new in us. We come into ourselves; we are grounded in that part of us which is most uniquely us; we arrive in our heart, but a greater heart than we had been able to feel before. For the heart, which sometimes seems to function as no more than the center of our own egoistic concerns, has currents running from it into the hearts of all other people in the world, as well as to the souls of those who have died, to higher spiritual beings, and through all the kingdoms of Nature. Some matters cannot really be discussed unless this greater heart has been developed to some extent. Some things sound ridiculous when one hears about them with normal day-to-day faculties, but when a current passes from the heart of one person into another (as I hope has by now been established between you and me as we work together on this book) then mysteries can be hinted at. If the sixth stage has been passed to some extent, those on the path should have a feeling of being connected to the world and at the same time feel grounded in their own creative heart.

The seventh stage is still to come, but we can say here that it signifies the new qualities that have begun to be formed into the Earth. It is sometimes given the name *rubedo* (reddening) and is also known as the *royal marriage*. The symbolism of a wedding is used because a marriage is made between Heaven and Earth, two spheres that are initially very dissimilar. By treading the path, inner receptivity has been created, and the way for the bridegroom to approach his beloved has been cleared. He approaches, and the spiritual works deep into body and soul.

Now that we have the whole sequence of the seven stages, we can also perceive and feel how they interrelate. With four as a kind of fulcrum, this sixth step is opposite to the second (as the first is to the seventh and the third is to the fifth). Some of the themes introduced in the second chapter find their "(re)solution" in the sixth. In chapter 2, it was recommended that the reader practice negative capability and endure the emptiness without giving in to premature solutions offered by addiction and fundamentalism. Now in chapter 6 the results of doing this can be appreciated. Those who resisted addiction acquired new abilities as a result. Such people will stand more strongly in command of their own life and possess a greater capacity to love. This will have been accomplished as a direct result of the negative capability practiced earlier.

Addiction arises when we satisfy a desire that is not yet purified, one that does not serve the whole being of body, soul, and spirit. Desire for food can healthily serve all three when it is directed at restoring the nutrition of the body that is the vehicle for soul and spirit. However, if the desire goes too much into the realm of culinary delight and stimulation of the palate, or if substances are taken in that are of poor nutritional value, or if more is consumed than the body needs, then there is a tendency for the desires of the soul to overpower the good health of body and spirit, and the balance of the three to be lost.

Whenever there is a push toward the enjoyment of the soul at the expense of the other faculties, an addiction has arisen. This can be said of any desire that demands enjoyment for satisfaction at the expense of other human beings or the environment. The world is not really so very separate from our own self as deluded, reductionist consciousness would have us believe. When we harm others or anything in our environment, even if we are completely unaware that this is happening, we actually harm ourselves. Many of our desires, such as that for food, are a mixture of addictive and non-addictive factors. When we experience a desire that, if acted on, takes us out of balance with ourselves, we are confronted by the choice in chapter 2: whether to practice negative capability and work toward that desire's purification or surrender to it and lose a bit of our freedom in the process. There are no firm rules in this; on the path to freedom, we each create our own point of balance between spirit and matter at every moment of life.

Behind any addictive desire is a force pushing you to take something into yourself that cannot really be yours. All sorts of criminal or unfree actions come from a person giving in to such forces. But behind these forces is something else: genuine desire for a deeper connection to the world. When those who suffer addictive desire simply surrender to it as it appears to them, the force works in a twisted way as a kind of longing for something that might or might not be satisfied in the future. However, if such people not only resist the desire but also manage to gain insight into the deeper realm from which the desire originates, the desire begins to change and reveal its hidden reality. When we practice this inner resistance to the forces that play into our life, and if we learn not to lose the intensity of the desire but to purify it through negative capability, the desire will lose its negative, harmful quality and start to work instead in its true form. It becomes something greater than it was before, the power that works in the world that we call love.

One of the images of the major arcana of the Tarot offers a picture of how we have the opportunity while on Earth to reject addiction and learn to love. Although the Tarot has become linked for many with fortune-telling and the like, just as alchemy has been linked with making gold, its images actually reflect universal truths that the soul encounters beyond the threshold. Contemplating the images and extracting meaning from them is a means to strengthen the soul and help it think in the kind of image-language that enables the spiritual world to become comprehensible.

The image to which I refer is related to this chapter and teaches us about love. It is the *sixth* major arcana of the Tarot. The same themes are dealt with in that image as in this chapter. In this version of the Tarot images, a young man is shown confronting two women who are each making him an offer; one promises him the gratifications of erotic love while the other, pointing away from herself, directs him to walk his spiritual path. The young man has a choice, the choice once more of chapter 2. The choice then was between something that would satisfy the desires but lead to an addiction, or something that would postpone gratification for a time and lead the soul into a process of inner development. That is the choice the man in the image must make.

Six is the number of love because two people who love each other purely meet as two complete individuals. In both men and women, when our love is pure, the bodily part is in balance with the great, vast, inner world of the soul, only a small portion of which we can be aware. Body and soul are in turn attuned to the great spiritual world to which they are connected, as by a fine thread, through their thinking. Individuals stand in their own individual threefold nature: three plus three. The coming together of their forces (symbolized imaginatively in the sixfold Star of David) offers great creative power.

When we experience attraction toward another person, our desire for something about that person can be gratified in different ways. We have animal drives and we have spiritual desires. We don't need to be moralistic about this; we simply need to be aware of the facts around this important law of our existence. The human being is indeed a strange bundle of opposing forces, and the greatest thing we can do in life is to set out upon the path to create within ourselves a higher harmony from their discord. Doing this is like learning to speak on a higher level; for the first time a person finds their true voice. At first, desire would tear apart the harmony of the threefold nature of one's inner being. The physical part or the soul part would overwhelm the spiritual part, for instance (though it can be just as bad, maybe worse, when the soul or bodily component is forcibly repressed by the spirit). Six is the number of love because it is the union of two complete, self-sustaining human beings—two people who are in balance within themselves and who, from this, come into balance with each other. The original meaning of the word *virgin* did not indicate one who hadn't yet had sexual intercourse, but someone who had the harmony of the three worlds within—one who is *complete*.

When a child is conceived, it makes a great difference if the two lovers are approaching this high goal, if they stand under the Star of David. If they do, their love will be no less intense than couples who are less balanced, but it will work so that something else can be active within it. In the Tarot image, this is symbolized by the child who is above. This could be the picture of a child conceived from the love of the two who are becoming its parents. Such a child might have a special grace; there might be less obstruction to fight through in life on the Earth than would another child whose parents created their child's earthly body without much sixfold harmony. The child of grace would be a "love child," entering the earthly path with unusual clarity about his or her destiny and calling.

But this image of lovers giving birth to a child is a picture of far more than the event of physical conception alone. All great transformation events are the result of an encounter between two people—or two forces—that have come into a relationship.

Transformation is also something that goes on entirely in solitude—an event between the masculine and feminine parts of a person. All soul transformation can work either destructively or creatively. Two members of a couple conflict with each other when processes are not managed judiciously. Likewise, individuals can come into equally terrible conflicts with themselves

Returning to physical love, if one of those "complete" human beings is a man and the other a woman what will happen if they come together in love? Many things could happen, but the hope for them would be that they are able to remain "complete" and in balance with themselves and each other, so that there is no compulsion involved and no loss in either individual of their inner integrity and harmony. Pure love may be physical or platonic—the outpouring to another of energy working on any or all of the levels of body, soul, and spirit. To become pure, the force of desire that stands behind love must to some extent have undergone a path of transformation. The greater the purification, the more blessed the love.

Was it easier in the past when people had guiding rules for when lovers may join together or a strict etiquette for courtship? Today such rules have almost completely disappeared in both East and West, and decisions are left more or less up to the couple, though there are those who would like to return to the clarity of earlier times. Has the whole business of love become easier because it is in the hands of the couple? How do we judge the degree to which love has been purified? Even if we are aware that love is a very high form of white magic and we wish to use it in the best way possible, how do we manage the processes of purification that will best serve a relationship? Such questions are not easy to answer. Mistakes will be made, from which we learn, but on the path we should maintain awareness of the need for harmony between ourselves and the world. In some parts of the world, this is known as cultivating awareness of *Dao* (or *Tao*) within. Presocratic Greek philosophy recognized it as inner guidance of the *Logos,* or Word. Whatever terminology we choose, we recognize the path as real and that it continuously attracts us if we are open to it.

The need to balance out the animal and the divine within us is a unique human situation. One is not meant to overpower the other—neither the animal overpowering the spiritual nor yet the spiritual overpowering or destroying the animal. Instead the two must find a harmony that arises from the spiritual part of us transforming and making peace with the animal part. The animal part is not something that is only negative. By transforming our desires these forces working within us are revealed for what they truly are. Although at first they may not seem this way at all, they are in essence holy. The playwright Anton Chekhov used to refer to himself as his own animal trainer. "Animal ennobler" would be nearer to the truth. We are not training animals within us (suppressing the inner animal); rather, we enable a progressive evolution of animal power within us so that our inner animal is raised to something greater. It is a long work and sometimes called the "great work," the *magnum opus.* It is gradual change and transformation, a drama hidden in each of our lives.

What of the other danger that chapter 2 describes? What happens if, through practicing negative capability, you are able to resist fundamentalism? Our yearning for certainty is very strong, and it is an act of heroism to turn away from easy answers and, without losing that yearning for knowledge, go into the arid desert of not knowing how long it will take. It recalls scientists who practice scientific method. They give all their attention to the phenomena at hand and, if they are real scientists, do not allow preexisting ideas (or the wishes of funders) to affect the results of their research. Religious people and scientists both practice something called *poverty;* it is not poverty in the sense of having few possessions but a refusal to apply preconceptions to what one encounters and the resolve to confront everything with a completely open and childlike sense of wonder. If you practice such an attitude toward the world, the gift that will come is the ability to see the world as a metaphor for the deep truths concealed in it. We do not see these truths at first because we perceive the world from the outside through our senses, but gradually we are empowered to go more deeply into the sacred mysteries of phenomena.

In this world, we generally view phenomena to begin with in a materialistic way. We see a tree and take it for a tree. We may not see a black border around the tree as in a children's coloring book, but we generally relate to the tree as though a border exists. We see it as a "tree," separate from everything else in the world. To think differently would be inconvenient, but our world is composed of solid matter and subtle forces. Our awareness of the world of objects must be balanced by an appreciation of life that includes the subtle as well as the visible and obvious. Materialism alone is insufficient.

Is spiritualism, then, what we should be practicing? To take up a style of thinking that is entirely *not of this world* is not the spiritual path. We live in a physical body for a reason, and the specifically human challenge is to bridge spirit and matter. The link between the two must be established in our consciousness; it is found by gradually transforming our thinking to become more flexible and mobile. We learn to experience the world of fixed objects and the world of subtle forces simultaneously by developing certain qualities of our heart. Our thinking needs to become imaginative, which arises by learning to use the power of metaphor. Artists and poets are very familiar with metaphor, but it should also become prevalent in life for spiritual seekers and scientists.

Just as *learning to love* is the solution to the problem of addiction, similarly *learning to perceive metaphors* solves the problem of fundamentalism. Those who walk the path and do not succumb to the easy temptation of fixed answers also learn to see metaphors in the sensory world. Behind everything we perceive is a message from across the threshold. When two people observe a rose, one may simply see a rose while the other has a secret premonition of the moment when the higher self will blossom. Two people watch the Moon rising over a lake; one sees only the Moon reflecting light from the Sun; the other sees a doorway into the mysteries of death and transformation. Every creeping beetle or child's smile signifies interactions between the infinite and the finite, a single letter in a script that we gradually decipher.

Symbolism and metaphor are the way the earthly part of us can relate to divine laws. The goal of the spiritual path, that event we call *initiation*, is something that has to be prepared over time because two worlds need to grow toward each other. The spiritual world is at first so unlike the world we experience with our senses that it is possible to have a spiritual experience and yet have no way to capture it in the memory or to communicate it to others.

When the British conspiracy theorist David Icke sees reptilian aliens, it is because he has perceived something partially genuine but misinterpreted it in a materialistic way. Accounts of alien abductions and the like can be understood in terms of something that happened to someone who has no way of relating to what actually took place without materialistic concepts. The world of spirit does not consist of fixed objects separated by boundaries; rather, it is a realm of dynamic circulation of moving energies.

Religious people are sometimes accused of anthropomorphizing everything—for example, building a picture of God in the image of one's earthly father. To see God as a man with a white beard is the product of a primitive imagination, but there is a link between the transient phenomena of this world and the powers that work into it from the eternal. The true relationship between the bound and the boundless is the exact opposite of how it is usually perceived. Phenomena of this world actually reflect the beings that hold sway in the spiritual sphere. The father we know on Earth is a kind of substitute for the Divine—one that will never make it to the standard of the original principle that works throughout the spiritual world. Likewise, another principle that actively nurtures and builds physical forms on Earth is called the Mother, and earthly mothers do their best to personify this activity with the children entrusted to them.

Goethe says at the end of *Faust,* "*Alles vergängliche ist nur ein Gleichnis*"[5] (All that is transient is but a parable), describing the invisible worlds that surround and uphold us. Being able to think in symbols (not in a riot of chaotic, clever mental associations but in a way that draws the two worlds together truthfully) is absolutely necessary for anyone on the path. Two worlds gradually approach each other; the spiritual seeker gradually and inexorably approaches the realm the heart desires to know.

We are weaving things together in this chapter—calling in the lost lambs, making ready our own marriage garment, preparing for the experience of the unity of life that is the final destination of this alchemical journey. Of course, it is an illusion if we think that we are going to reach a fixed destination; no matter what we achieve, all must be continually won anew at ever-deeper levels. Still, moments of rest and reflection are given to us. We resolved in early chapters that we would seek fulfillment in our own individual life "without falling into the aberrations of either fundamentalism or addiction, ignorance or despair." Fulfillment is not something we find at the very end of our journey after long misery. Fulfillment is something that can be felt at all moments, even in times of pain and loss. Gratitude for all we have been given, thankfulness for being allowed to travel this path, even through its difficulties and dangers, can be a constant underlying mood of the soul, much as the blue sky is always there, though concealed by clouds, or like the stars in daytime. These are simple images, but if you don't absorb their inner meaning into yourself and become like nature herself, you will find it difficult to maintain your sense of proportion and your way. A sense of humor is also quite important. The drama of the interaction between the eternal and the "human, all too human," can be both comic and tragic. There are qualities in every one of us that are just so incongruous with the eternal aspects of our deeper being, and, when we are able to appreciate the humorous side of things, we are far more able to cope with life under these strange earthly conditions than those who do not.

This sixth chapter is intended to bring greater awareness of the eternal to our feeling life. Our heart knows. "One who possesses science and art also has religion. One who has neither of these— *Let that one have religion!*" said that audacious poet Goethe.[6] We who walk the path need to unite the clarity and reverence for life of the true scientist with the inner sensitivity of the artist. We need to become poets to the mysteries of life that are constantly weaving around and through us. Only artists can appreciate and do justice to the infinite. Our heart knows only when it has passed through a transformation that unites it with qualities of the head. Meanwhile the head passes through its own transformation and becomes capable of following movement and process and understanding quality rather than thinking only in static, brain-bound forms.

A Shakespeare character speaks in *A Midsummer Night's Dream* (act 5, sc. 1) of the similarities among "the lunatic, the lover, and the poet." There are risks along the path, which the lunatic personifies. Taken slowly, step by step, we become lovers and poets; we acquire what the French philosopher Henri Bergson called *élan vital* ("vital impetus"), because we live at the growing point of life and our sap is green whatever our chronological age may be. And the final step upon this path of knowledge will bring us into a profound unity of action with the entire Earth. On the axis of love, when it is strong enough, we can go down deeper than the heart. First there is the open mind, then the open heart; the final stage will be the open will.[7] When love is planted into the earth and takes root there, then it is inevitable that something of value will result from this. The fruits of our labors may turn out not to have been done for ourselves at all, but this is not our concern. Though what we achieved may have been something that cost us a great deal at the time we did it and though it may have taken all our strength to carry this through, we will not be troubled by this. Knowing the interconnectedness of humanity, we feel a simple joy in having achieved something that will be of benefit to those who come after us. We have done our work simply because we loved doing it.

SUMMARY OF CHAPTER 6: THE HEART KNOWS

The sixth stage of the journey has to do with the wholeness of the heart, or heart thinking. Overview of all seven stages:

Stage 1. Undifferentiated elements in our soul life

Stage 2. Separation. Learning to endure the pain of negative capability and to resist the temptations of premature gratification through addiction and fundamentalism

Stage 3. Fusion of separate elements into something new. The new ability to carry thoughts across the threshold

Stage 4. Meeting the forces of death

Stage 5. The softening, dissolving process of letting go

Stage 6. Condensation of what is new in us; arriving in our heart in a way in which we are able to feel the currents that connect us to the hearts of others, to the spiritual world and to the kingdoms of Nature

Stage 7. The royal marriage, Earth and Heaven coming together

The sixth stage connects to the second in such a way that the person who practiced negative capability in the second stage is able to acquire a greater capacity to love in the sixth. The sixth major arcana of the Tarot is a picture of the overcoming of addiction by attaining the capacity to love. Six is the number of love—the unification of two entities that are each complete in their threefold nature. Love is the power that makes possible the transformation of the animal part of us.

Just as love is the solution to addiction, imagination—thinking transformed by the heart to become subtle, mobile, and able to grasp living spiritual thought—is the solution to fundamentalism. Through imagination the world becomes a metaphor that points to the realities that lie behind it. The metaphor shows us the connection between earthly and spiritual realities. What is on Earth is an image of what is eternal rather than vice versa. Being able to think in symbols draws the two worlds truthfully together.

Thankfulness and a sense of humor on the path. The heart that knows. "Only artists can appreciate and do justice to the infinite." Pure love that is free from wanting any kind of reward for oneself can be the motivation for what a person does.

7

Freedom, the Final Frontier

"Verum, sine mendacio, certum et verissimum.
Quod est inferius, est sicut quod est superius, et quod est
superius, est sicut quod est inferius, ad perpetranda mirac-
ula rei unius."

(True it is, without falsehood, certain and most true.
That which is above is like to that which is below, and that
which is below is like to that which is above, to accomplish
the miracles of the one thing.)

—THE EMERALD TABLET[1]

"The human being is the higher sense of our planet—the star
which connects it with the upper world, the eye which it
turns toward Heaven."

—NOVALIS[2]

"For man represents Nature toward God, and he represents
God toward Nature."

—ANONYMOUS, *Meditations on the Tarot*[3]

"For the creation waits with eager longing for the revealing
of the sons of God; for the creation was subjected to futil-
ity...in the hope that the creation itself will be set free from
its bondage to decay and obtain the glorious liberty of the
children of God. We know that the whole creation has been
suffering the pangs of childbirth until now."

—ST. PAUL[4]

The seven chapters in this book are one person's attempt to help readers remain on their path to experience the opening heart and consecration of the will. If this book has been read in such a way that you *lived* what you read and the content did not just stay in your head, then an exchange of energy has taken place between your head and heart. The heart, our wonderful organ of human creativity, is on an evolutionary path to becoming an organ that perceives truth and from which we can act with inner, unforced initiative. Before this can happen, the heart must learn to think, become clear and objective, and grow in strength. This will happen through an alliance between heart and head. Such an alliance is not a one-way affair, since the head will also change. In response to the heart, the head will cease being an organ only of brain-bound intellectuality and assume some of the heart's qualities. It becomes more creative and its thoughts grow life-filled and warm.

People who have begun to awaken the *axis of creative love* between head and heart will be those who have dared to take their particular path into the unknown. The path in previous centuries was open only to a few, but now calls to many. "The gate is narrow and the way is hard that leads to life. And those who find it are few."[5] Results are not instant and one must persevere and remain patient in an entirely new orientation. It is easier to leave the path and digress into alluring and intoxicating areas of addiction and fundamentalism. Avoiding the easy road, however, becomes increasingly fulfilling. We discover who we really are, take hold of the eternal part within us, and learn to express this in our everyday encounters in life.

This is a path to freedom that lives as longing—seldom expressed truthfully—in everyone. Real inner freedom is not the license and opportunity to do whatever you want; rather, it is the ability to act from a center of creative initiative that is instinctively in tune with everything taking place in the world at that moment. It is the ability to connect with the spirit of the times and to serve the evolutionary current of our age. Very many voices today are telling you this cannot be done—that you are doomed always to follow only your hormones, conditioning, self-interest, or the will of those stronger than you. Such ideas are born of reductionism. Freedom is possible. Much that we do in daily life *is* done because of hormones and conditioning, self-concern, or obedience to social norms or laws, but on the path of inner development these external imperatives gradually fall away. This assertion cannot be an article of dogma—it can only be experienced. Those who tread the path will know from personal experience that it is possible because they will find it happening in their own life; those who do not will continue to assert that what I say is a fabrication that simply replaces one kind of egoism with another.

Throughout this account of the path the importance of the phenomenon of the threshold has been emphasized. The threshold is the dynamic field of force that one meets at the point where conventional thinking loses its power. Approaching it, chaotic energy that will split the personality is unleashed into a person's life. In one who is not prepared, this can bring about all sorts of aberrations or mental illnesses, which is why humanity was in the past protected and prohibited from moving beyond the orbit of the sense-perceptible world. Institutions such as the Catholic Church worked to hold human beings back from experiences that had the potential to destroy them.

Today, many of these archaic forms of protection are gone. More and more people are impelled toward the threshold; it comes toward them and they feel with an inner necessity that they *must* cross. Usually this encounter with the threshold takes place in deep unconsciousness, but its effects are felt. That it is happening is one reason for the disintegration of social forms we witness daily. Only special attention to the development of one's own faculties enables the crossing to be made in a conscious and healthy manner. Such attention is the path. In the twenty-first century some people need to prepare for a healthy crossing. They will experience inner changes at ever-deeper levels of their being. If they can bear crossing the threshold and stand within the light of the reality they encounter on the other side, they will inspire others toward them by a mighty power of attraction.

In time, all humanity will be increasingly drawn to cross the threshold. We cannot expect this to be easy or straightforward and there is much within us and in the world outside that does everything possible to stop it from happening in a healthy way. Human freedom is a very dangerous quality to those who do not want humanity to advance, for there is no greater power in the world than the human being who has become spiritually free. In chapter 4, we looked at the reactionary powers that strive toward a "new world order" that would keep human beings unfree and doing only the will of a small elite. Since then we have turned back toward ourselves, for it is in our own souls that the greatest changes can be made. However, our lives are not taking place in a social bubble, and all of us, in our many different ways, constantly interact with the world. As well as knowing ourselves we need to know this world and the forces that are working in it. It is time to determine what sort of relationship we should have with the powers hostile to freedom and to an orderly crossing of the threshold.

The fundamental expression of the will against the free human being is expressed in the sign of two fingers, whether it is the "V" sign of Sir Winston Churchill or the more recent "cool" sign made by extending thumb and little finger and closing the other three. In both cases a secret acknowledgement is given (whether or not the one making the sign is aware of it) that "two" is ruling "three."

The human being is a pentagram, but the upright pentagram is reversed when the two (two limbs as the instinctual part of our being) rule over the three (head and feeling life expressed in the two arms). Free human beings work from the axis of love living in mutually attuned head and heart, whereas unfree human beings are "led by the nose" and controlled by whatever driving force dominates at any given moment in their unconscious will.

Our will is free when it can receive its motivation from head and heart, motives that correspond to our deep wish to reconnect through love to the sources of one's primal life and being. When this happens then there exists, in addition to the axis of love mentioned earlier in this chapter, an *axis of creative initiative* that weaves among head, heart, and limbs. However for this to happen a degree of maturity is needed, with some experience of treading the path. Without walking the path, we cannot know what is working in our will, and we will be open to various sources of hindrance without realizing what is happening to us through them. Directing the will from what is highest in humanity is the very greatest challenge of the spiritual life. The will that strives to be free is challenged by everything connected with addiction in the feeling life and with fundamentalism in the thinking life. This third counter-force is active wherever there is any *enslavement* of the will.

Free individuals will lead very different kinds of lives from one another; what they do will be determined by their positions in life, their previous experiences, their karma. They can be members of any religion they choose, however they will be very careful in how they connect to mass groups where there is the danger of forces taking over their will and giving them motives which they have not freely chosen for themselves. There will always be mass movements that attempt to enslave human beings and make them conform in their actions to the will of one or more powerful individuals who manipulate them. What took place in Germany during the 1930s can happen anywhere again. We live constantly under the shadow of what wants to compel us to go in directions detrimental to humanity, and in our time the greatest cunning is exerted in making what is evil appear to be good and of benefit to all. The most reliable way to stand up to the power of this "spin" is to tread the path that brings self-knowledge.

Yet not everything that curtails a person's freedom is part of some overarching conspiracy against humanity. We meet opposition in many ways. Some of it is for our own correction and education and a reminder to us of the rights of others; some of it is a challenge that we must overcome for the good of the world. Sometimes it is not easy to tell different kinds of opposition apart. But the opposition against human progress—if we can distinguish it from the other kind—has its place in the world, and it is right that we meet it. There must be resistance in order for our wills to develop properly, for the will is made strong through "great aims, great examples, great opposition,"[6] and "what doesn't kill you makes you stronger."[7]

As stated in chapter 4 concerning 9/11, it was not my intention to give the full account of everything wicked in the world. We are called to work in different ways, some by confronting evil directly and others through subtle cultivation of the good. Not everyone needs to be concerned with understanding evil in all its depths; it is more important that we have an overview and are able to practice self-knowledge and resistance to what tries to compel us, and that we are able to become a channel for the good to work through us. This may happen in ways beyond our comprehension. There may be times when we need to go out of our way to resist injustice, but we are called also to do the quiet, inner work of maintaining equilibrium against opposition in ways that no one else will see. The path is a quiet affair and one that can be walked in very many different kinds of situations; it is probable that few people will even realize that we are walking it.

In the life of individuals on the path, crisis is the way we learn. Crisis takes place in the soul life of individuals, and crisis will take place, too, in the destiny of nations on Earth. People will be needed who will not lose heart in the face of great disintegration around them. Considerable presence of mind will be required to see within destruction a necessary part of creation and not be shattered by what one sees. Those who are able do this do so because they are in touch with the power of imagination in their hearts. They are able to create incentives to act that arise from their awareness of what is good for the entire Earth and not for themselves alone. Increasingly, the survival of the Earth will depend on the power and focus of energy expressed by these creative individuals.

Just as any idea starts in the head and must become a resolution taken into the will, so, too, theoretical ideas *about* the path must be put into practice. This chapter represents the experiences in the final stage of the alchemical path, called *The Royal Marriage.* Ideas need to deepen and enter the sphere of will and actively work in the place of power, the solar plexus. Of course, these changes do not happen all at once by reading a few pages of information, but these pages offer a taste of the seventh process and may help readers who have worked through the first six stages.

What are the changes taking place through human development that counteract social disintegration? One of these is a whole new humanization of the social structures of the world. Reductive science, government bureaucracy, and corporate power that serve the few at the expense of the many have created impersonal and destructive social forms. Although these forms have huge power over the lives of individuals, the activity of free human beings is the one and only thing that will transform them.

Today, much has been established to serve the interests of governments and corporations, but social structures must begin to serve everyone. Just as the basic human constitution is three-fold (limbs, trunk, and head), the structure of society needs to be differentiated into three parts. In most parts of the world today, both East and West, we see an unholy alliance of state and business interests. The world appears to us in the image of a criminal who is not free because that person is dominated by instinctive and destructive impulses living in the will.

Only through a kind of "people power" can that destructiveness of the will be blocked. Governments must be forced to focus on the rights of their citizens, not on what is good for government and its business partners. Hope for the world depends on ordinary human beings awaking to their power to change the course of history. Free human beings have the potential to wield the greatest power for change in civil society. When they are active and are clear about what they are doing, civil society will be able to separate state and corporate interests and eliminate the destructive power of an economic system that serves only "the one percent." Led by free human beings, civil society can be the balance between state and corporation. When it is strong it can steer government away from financial dealing and toward its true task of protecting the rights of its citizens.[6]

It is to be expected that vested interests in government and corporate life will wage war against this. Increasingly, corrupt governments and corporations pose the greatest hinderance to what is good for humanity. The attack on human freedom begins at birth, and many educational practices today are little more than methods to stunt and destroy the human mind, heart, and will. In the merger of government and corporation there are individuals who do all they can to distract, divide, and confuse people. Countless examples are everywhere. There appear to be plans, for instance, for a body that will act as a kind of United Nations of the spiritual life to monitor and control what people in different faiths are permitted to think and practice together. However all these maneuvers against spiritual freedom only prove its importance. The fundamental power of civil society is the free individual. Even when terrible things are happening in the rest of society, individuals anywhere can quietly develop the power to sow seeds of transformation in society. Individuals simply need to find their creative center and, from this, connect with others.

Associations of all kinds create civil society. Individuals become more powerful than they could ever imagine when they unite with others in a shared objective, in harmony with the needs of the times. A true globalization is founded not upon huge conglomerations such as the IMF, the World Bank, and the Bank for International Settlements, each one of which was put in place to serve special interests, but upon individuals whose hearts are linked to others.

Everything today is set up to benefit big organizations, to the degree that it is difficult to imagine individuals being able to wield significant power in the world. Members of the global elite work out of deep structures of power to produce a society in their own image and in the spirit of Macbeth's desire:

> I had else been perfect,
> Whole as marble, founded as the rock,
> As broad and general as the casing air.[7]

People exist who, working consciously or unconsciously against human freedom, serve the dream of an empire akin to that of Macbeth. The system of control they desire resembles a kingdom of ants or termites, in which each insect mindlessly goes about its task with no thought for what is being achieved. Human spiritual life follows laws that work quite differently from those employed by those who would use power in this way. The light that works through free human beings brings about a very different kind of society; it is the lives of such human beings that make Macbeth's dream impossible.

In the sphere of the spiritual life, individuals wield power— even when this is not visible—when they work with others and when their activity has attained enough potency. It is only in this sense that we can understand the influence of men such as Mahatma Gandhi, and Dr. Martin Luther King Jr. They were remarkable human beings, certainly, but they wanted others to find their own inner genius and become remarkable, as well. They internalized something of the divine within them. Through them a creative power, working constantly to create higher life out of the forces of death and decay, has entered into the world. As a certain critical mass is reached in the ability for individuals to transcend their conditioning and their national characteristics and to become bearers of the divine will, the world will change. It will change as a reflection of the changes that have taken place within these individuals. Gandhi's saying "Be the change you wish to see in the world"[8] is deeply significant. If you set about changing the world by hurling Molotov cocktails at it, you work out of the destructive energies of your own soul and you will bring only destruction. If you see what is lacking in the world around you and incarnate into yourself the part of it that is lacking, then the world will be changed by your activity.

The great slogan that describes how to work effectively in the world is to "think globally and act locally." In the sphere of the spiritual life there is an equivalent saying: *"Think eternally and BE HERE NOW!"* We act entirely as individuals, but in our actions the values of an eternal reality are brought into the ordinary, physical world. When the sphere of eternity is linked to this world, everything changes and evolves. Freedom does not mean acting on fixed principles; rather, freedom takes place when we find unique solutions that originate in the eternal, the realm of Truth. Nevertheless, what creative individuals draw from it will be tailored to respond perfectly to the specific earthly situations we face. People who allow the breath of the eternal to come into their daily life will have the presence of mind to act freely in response to each new situation. They won't just be "God's spies," his eyes and ears, but his arms and legs and larynx, as well.

It was stated in chapter 3 that human beings have three signs (our capacities for thought, language, and standing upright), by which our spiritual origin can be traced. If we are going to become free individuals, each of these three capacities needs to be transformed from what is given to us in the first years of life. At about twelve months most of us learned how to stand. However, our ability to transform this into real inner freedom takes much longer. To stand in the highest sense is to have learned to be able to create and work out of the axis of creative initiative that works between our head, heart and will. With people in many lands successfully undergoing the difficult transition of learning to live without the support systems of previous times, I believe we are justified in having a certain optimism about the future of the Earth despite all the attacks that are being waged upon free thought. To walk the path is to fight through to the point where thought becomes free of fundamentalist dogma and feeling is unchained from addictions and compulsions. Having been liberated from everything that enslaves it, the will can do what is truly good. Although there is undoubtedly great evil and manufactured chaos today, and although the situation is likely to become worse before it gets better, the attraction of the power of good is irresistible. A breakthrough from one person exerts influence far beyond what can be measured.

In chapter 2, I quoted from a letter of Katherine Mansfield, in which she described her realization of a need to go forward into a completely different kind of creative will. She lived only three years after writing that, dying at the age of thirty-four. However, about three months before her death she described in her journal the kind of human being she was endeavoring to be. She writes of something that all who take up the path may feel, a quality that radiates toward us from the future but works actively within us now. Katherine Mansfield's words conclude this little book about the spiritual path:

> I want to enter into [the world], to be part of it, to live in it, to learn from it, to lose all that is superficial and acquired in me and to become a conscious, direct human being. I want, by understanding myself, to understand others. I want to be all that I am capable of becoming so that I may be (and here I have stopped and waited and waited and it's no good—there's only one phrase that will do) a child of the Sun.[9]

Always They Come

This is the path
where you can plunge into the abyss
and rise up three days later
with the scent of roses on your breath.

Who is there who believes in the path today?
Who walks the path today?
Always they come
whose names are called.

Always they yearn
for what they never will be able to possess
unless all that belongs to death in them
is given back to death.

And then, through them,
creative power will work
to transform chaos, decay, and death
to pure, abundant life.

      (MB, previously unpublished)

SUMMARY OF CHAPTER 7:
FREEDOM, THE FINAL FRONTIER

The interaction of head and heart—how the heart learns objectivity and becomes capable of thinking while the head learns warmth and becomes life-giving and creative. The axis of creative love between head and heart. Freedom as the ability to act out of a center of creative initiative that is instinctively in tune with everything that is taking place in the world.

Crossing the threshold means enduring a breakdown in the power of ordinary thinking and becoming subject to forces that split the personality. Walking the path is preparing oneself to be able to endure exposure to these forces with no damage resulting to oneself or others. In our time many of the protective social forms and prohibitions that shielded human beings from feeling the destructive effects of these forces are breaking down, and this is one reason why society, too, is breaking down. The world needs individuals who can make the crossing without being destroyed by the forces that are released when this happens.

The seventh stage of the alchemical process is about ideas that have been deepened until they come into the sphere of the will. It is part of our task to counteract social disintegration and create new social structures to replace those that have of necessity been destroyed. A new modeling of society based on the same threefold structure that is present in the human being. Free human beings who work within civil society can drive a wedge between the unholy alliance of corporations and governments. Gandhi's words: "Be the change you wish to see in the world." "If you set about changing the world by hurling Molotov cocktails at it, you work out of the destructive energies of your own soul and you will bring only destruction. If you see what is lacking in the world around you and incarnate into yourself the part of it that is lacking, then the world will be changed by your activity." Learning how to act so that eternal values are incarnated through your actions. The power of good to attract. Final quotation from Katherine Mansfield—to be "a child of the Sun." Poem, "Always They Come."

Notes

Introduction

1. Dag Hammarskjöld: *Markings*. London: Faber and Faber, 1964.
2. Valentin Andreae, "The Chymical Wedding," in *A Christian Rosenkreutz Anthology* (compiled by Paul Marshall Allen), Great Barrington, MA: SteinerBooks, 2000.

Chapter 1: The Starting Point

1. Herman Hesse, *Steppenwolf.* London: Penguin, 1974.
2. William Golding, *The Inheritors*. London: Faber and Faber, 1976. For another book that shows the gradual change of consciousness of humanity, read David Wansbrough, *A Pillar of Salt?* Woolloomooloo, NSW, Australia: Print Room, 1988.

Chapter 2: What Is Happening in the Soul?

1. Antonio Machado, "Proverbios y cantares XXIX," in *Campos de Castilla*, Madrid: Cátedra, 2006.
2. *Being Beethoven*, unpublished play by M. Burton, 2003.
3. See, for example Lindsay Clarke, *Parsifal and the Stone from Heaven: A Grail Romance Retold for Our Time,* London: HarperCollins, 2001.
4. St. John of the Cross, *The Dark Night of the Soul*, Cambridge, UK: James Clark, 1973.
5. Katherine Mansfield, Letter of Nov. 16, 1919. In *Letters and Journals* (ed. C. K. Stead), London: Allen Lane, 1977.
6. J. B. Priestley, *An Inspector Calls* (New York: Dramatists Play Service, 1998) "If men will not learn that lesson [that they are responsible for each other], then they will be taught it in fire and blood and anguish" (from the final speech of Inspector Goole).
7. Erich Fromm, *To Have or to Be?* London: Jonathan Cape, 1978, p. 17.

8. Thomas Henry Huxley, *On the Advisableness of Improving Natural Knowledge*, 1866.

9. Shakespeare, *Hamlet*, Act I, scene 3. It is Ophelia who speaks the phrase while opposing the views of her brother, Laertes.

10. John Davy suggests in his wonderful, unpublished continuation of C. S. Lewis, *The Screwtape Letters,* that one of the best techniques in the armory of infernal technology employed by all devils is contained in the much-repeated phrase, "You can't change human nature!" See John Davy, *Screwtape Continued,* unpublished, 1979.

11. Hermann Hesse, *op cit.*

12. From "Australia Needs a New Financial System, Based on Glass-Steagall and a National Bank," in *The New Citizen*, Nov./Dec. 2014. The figures quoted were correct for one of the banks (ANZ) at the time of printing.

13. "...when a man is capable of being in uncertainties, Mysteries, doubts, without any irritable reaching after fact or reason." John Keats, letter to his brothers George and Tom, Dec. 22, 1817, in *Selected Letters*, Oxford, UK: Oxford World's Classics, 2002.

14. *The boundary of the bearable* is an expression from the book by Bernhard J. Lievegoed, *Toward the Twenty-first Century: Doing the Good in the Twenty-first Century,* N. Vancouver: Steiner Book Centre, 1972.

Chapter 3: The Nature of the Threshold

1. Quoted in Wilhelm Rath, *The Friend of God from the Highlands*, Stroud UK: Hawthorn Press.

2. Hermann Hesse, *op cit.*

3. Charles Darwin: *The Origin of Species*, 1858. Compare these words of four paragraphs earlier: "To my mind it accords better with what we know of the laws impressed on matter by the Creator that the production and extinction of the past and present inhabitants of the world should have been due to secondary causes like those determining the birth and death of the individual."

4. P. Senge, C. O. Scharmer, et al., *Presence: Human Purpose and the Field of the Future* (The Society for Organizational Learning, Cambridge, MA, 2004), pp. 204f. "The reductionist approach to the problem [of how plants grow from simple embryos into the characteristic form of their species] is to say that all morphogenesis is genetically programmed. Yet, Sheldrake wondered, if all cells have the same genetic programming, how do they develop so differently? This question drove him to imagine a radical alternative:

that invisible blueprints he called 'morphic fields' underlie the form of growing organisms. For 'self-organizing systems at all levels of complexity, there is a wholeness that depends on a characteristic organizing field of that system. Each self-organizing system is a whole made up of parts, which are themselves whole at a lower level. At each level, the morphic field gives each whole its characteristic properties and makes it more than the sum of its parts.'"

5.   Rudolf Steiner, *How to Know Higher Worlds: A Modern Path of Initiation* (tr. A. Zajonc, Hudson, NY: Anthroposophic Press, 1994); previous translations include *The Way of Initiation: How to Attain Knowledge of the Higher Worlds* (Mokelumne Hill, CA: Mokelumne Hill Press, 1960) and *Knowledge of the Higher Worlds and Its Attainment* (tr. G. Metaxa, New York: Anthroposophic Press, 1947). The *Roadmap* is nowhere near as exact a path as this book, which is really the definitive text for people who wish seriously to take up the path of initiation. I would suggest that all travelers on the path can profit by referring to it and treating it as a kind of technical manual for spiritual growth. In particular regarding this chapter and the two to come, see Steiner's outline of the basic conditions for esoteric training (chapter entitled "The Conditions of Esoteric Training") and his descriptions of the threshold and its crossing (see "Some Effects of Initiation" and "The Guardian of the Threshold").

    A parallel work by Steiner that is very much related to the path of the *Roadmap* is his book *The Philosophy of Freedom,* sometimes titled *The Philosophy of Spiritual Activity* (as Steiner himself suggested), and the most recent translation published as *Intuitive Thinking as a Spiritual Path: A Philosophy of Freedom* (tr. M. Lipson, Hudson, NY: Anthroposophic Press, 1995); and *The Philosophy of Freedom* (tr. M. Wilson, London: Rudolf Steiner Press, 1963). Like *How to Know Higher Worlds*, written at the start of the twentieth century, this is an example of the kind of heart thinking aimed for in the *Roadmap* and can stimulate in readers who work with it a similar process of development as is outlined here.

Chapter 4: Into the Labyrinth

1.   Erich Fromm, *op cit.*

2.   St. Paul, Eph. 6:12.

3.   Johann von Goethe, *Sayings of Goethe Translated: The Maxims and Reflections of Goethe* (tr. B. Saunders), New York: Macmillan, 1893.

4. Dietrich Bonhoeffer, *Letters and Papers from Prison,* New York: Macmillan, 1962.

5. Rudolf Steiner, *The Way of Initiation,* page 67.

6. The website "Architects and engineers for 9/11 Truth" is at http://www.ae911truth.org.

7. David Ray Griffin, *The New Pearl Harbor: Disturbing Questions about the Bush Administration and 9/11* (Northampton, MA: Olive Branch, 2004); *The 9/11 Commission Report: Omissions and Distortions* (Olive Branch, 2005); see also "Flights 11, 175, 77, and 93: The 9/11 Commission's Incredible Tales" (Dec. 5, 2005, http://www.911truth.org/article.php?story=20051205150219651); "The Destruction of the World Trade Center: Why the Official Account Cannot Be True" (http://911review.com/articles/griffin/nyc1.html).

8. Steven E. Jones. "Why Indeed Did the WTC Buildings Collapse?" (Nov. 11, 2005, http://www.infowars.com/articles/sept11/wtc_buildings_collapse_steven_jones.htm).

9. Mike Ruppert, *Crossing the Rubicon: The Decline of the American Empire at the End of the Age of Oil,* Gabriola Island, BC: New Society, 2004.

10. Attributed to Jean Paul Getty.

11. See Stephan Mögle-Stadel, *Dag Hammarskjöld. Visionary for the Future of Humanity,* South Africa: Novalis, 1999.

12. Zbigniew Brzezinski, *The Grand Chessboard: American Primacy and Its Geostrategic Imperatives* (New York: Basic, 1997), p. 40.

13. Dag Hammarskjöld, "The Walls of Distrust," address at Cambridge University, June 5, 1958, in A. W. Cordier/Wilder Foote (eds): *Public Papers of the Secretaries-General of the United Nations. Volume IV, Dag Hammarskjöld 1958–1960* (New York: Columbia University, 1974), pp. 90f and 91f. In that address Hammarskjöld said, "The widening of our political horizons to embrace in a new sense the whole of the world, should have meant an approach to the ideal sung in Schiller's *Ode to Joy,* but it has, paradoxically, led to new conflicts and to new difficulties to establish even simple human contact and communication."

14. "The old order changeth yielding place to new. And God fulfills himself in many ways lest one good practice should corrupt the whole." Alfred Lord Tennyson, *Morte d'Arthur,* 1830.

15. Shakespeare, *The Tempest.* Act V, sc. 1, 275f.

16. Goethe, see in P. M. Allen and J. D. Allen, *The Time Is at Hand: The Rosicrucian Nature of Goethe's Fairy Tale of the Green Snake*

and the Beautiful Lily and the Mystery Dramas of Rudolf Steiner, Hudson, NY: Anthroposophic Press, 1995.

17. Dag Hammarskjöld, *op cit.*
18. Pierre Teilhard de Chardin, *The Phenomenon of Man,* 1955.

CHAPTER 5: CROSS NOW!

1. *The Green Snake* by M. Burton; play based on Goethe's *Fairy Tale,* performed by The Mask Studio, 1998 (Stroud, UK: Hawthorn Press, 2000).

2, 3. Goethe and Pratanjali (in *Yoga Sutras*), quoted in Anonymous, *Meditations on the Tarot,* "Letter I," New York: Putnam, 1985.

4. Lines from a verse often given as *For the Michael Age* by Rudolf Steiner. The verse is actually a compendium from three different sources—all by Rudolf Steiner but in three different places. The lines in question were supposedly by Steiner to Emanuel Zeylmans van Emmichoven. See Barry Lia at http://www.mail-archive .com/bdnow@envirolink.org/msg04857.html. Although not quite the same as if the verse had originated from a single source, the thoughts expressed are so relevant to the overall message of the *Roadmap* that I'd like to give the full text:

> We must eradicate from the soul
> all fear and terror of what comes to us from the future.
> We must acquire serenity
> in all feelings and sensations about the future.
> We must look forward with absolute equanimity
> to everything that may come.
> And we must think only that whatever comes
> is given to us by a world directive full of wisdom.
>
> It is part of what we must learn in this age—
> namely to live out of pure trust
> without any security in existence,
> trust in that ever-present help of the spiritual world.
>
> Truly, nothing else will do
> if our courage is not to fail us.
>
> Let us discipline our will.
> And let us seek this awakening within ourselves
> every morning and every evening.

5.   Dag Hammarskjöld, *op cit.*

6.   The account is given in Matt. 14:23–33, Mark 6:47–51, and John 6:16–21. See also Frederick Rittlemeyer, *Meditation: Letters on the Guidance of the Inner Life.* Aberdeen, UK: University Press, 1948. This book uses St. John's Gospel as material for meditation, and in chapter 11 takes the event of walking on water as a meditation against fear and weakness.

7.   The last three lines of a meditation given by Rudolf Steiner in *Verses and Meditations* (tr. G. and M. Adams. London: Rudolf Steiner Press, 2004.

Chapter 6: The Heart Knows

1.   Michael Chekhov, recorded talks to actors; available as *Michael Chekhov: On Theatre and the Art of Acting: The Five-Hour Master Class, 4 CDs and Booklet* (Milwaukee: Applause Theatre & Cinema, 2004; ISBN: 978-1-55783-531-4).

2.   Dylan Thomas, *The force that through the green fuse drives the flower.* In *Dylan Thomas: The Poems.* London; J. M. Dent, 1971.

3.   Matt. 10:16.

4.   Paul Marshall Allen, *op cit.*

5.   "All things transitory are but a parable." Goethe: *Faust*, Part II, act 5, 12, 104f.

6.   Johann von Goethe, *"Zahme Xenien" IX, Goethes Gedichte in Zeitlicher Folge,* Berlin: Insel Verlag 1982.

7.   This comes from the work of Otto Scharmer. See http://www .ottoscharmer.com/bio and www.presencing.com.

Chapter 7: Freedom, the Final Frontier

1.   *The Emerald Tablet (in Proceedings of the Royal Society of Medicine xxi, 1928, translated by Robert Steele and Dorothy Singer);* quoted in Anonymous, *Meditations on the Tarot,* "Letter I."

2.   Novalis, *Fragments,* in Thomas Carlyle: *Critical and Miscellaneous Essays,* vol. 2, New York: Scribner's, 1904.

3.   *Meditations on the Tarot, op cit,* "Letter XX."

4.   Rom. 8:19–23.

5.   Matt. 7:14.

6.   Friedrich Rittelmeyer, *Meditation: Guidance of the Inner Life,* Floris Books, 2012.

7.   Friedrich Nietzsche, *Twilight of the Idols,* 1888

8. See Nicanor Perlas: *Shaping Globalization: Civil Society, Cultural Power and Threefolding.* Quezon City, Philippines: Centre for Alternative Development Initiatives, 2000.

9. Shakespeare, *Macbeth,* act 3, sc. 4.

10. As a number of people have pointed out, there is no evidence Gandhi ever said exactly this, though his grandson says he heard him say it fifty years earlier. The saying could be a shortening of something Gandhi did once say, "If we could change ourselves, the tendencies in the world would also change. As a man changes his own nature, so does the attitude of the world change toward him.... We need not wait to see what others do" (opinion piece by Brian Morton, *New York Times*, Aug. 29, 2011).

11. Katherine Mansfield: Journal entry of Oct. 14, 1922, in *The Journal of Katherine Mansfield* (1927), New York: Ecco, 1983.

www.ingramcontent.com/pod-product-compliance
Lightning Source LLC
Chambersburg PA
CBHW020914090426
42736CB00008B/627